JUST stitch

Lesley Turpin-Delport   Nikki Delport-Wepener

Authors' acknowledgements

We wish to thank all the fabulous needlecraft and creative friends who have contributed to this book. There are so many wonderful people that we have worked with over the past decade it would be impossible to thank everyone individually but special mention and thanks go to:

Marion Berkowitz, Elaine Cohen, Pat Erasmus and her daughter Kim Hugo, Daleen, Nancy Gardiner, Elaine Goldberg, Shirley Hirshberg, Claire Lang, Lesley Lewis, Carol Light, Hazel Metz, Wilsia Metz and her family, Malka Meister, Ivan Naudé, Anne Neill, Dr Tom Ombrello, Mandy Rosenbaum, Chava Tachelet, Mike Tarpey, Ray Wepener, Mike Young

Creative inspiration credits

Wonderful paintings and pictures from artists past and present: Barbara Pike, Bernard Durin, J. Mulder Sculp & Maria Sibylla Merian 1647-1717, P. Barichievy, Renoir 19th Century, Robert Furber 1730, Walter Hood Fitch 1817-1892.

Every attempt has been made to acknowledge the inspiration for the stitched pieces. Where the attempt has been unsuccessful, we would be pleased to hear from the source so any omission or error can be rectified.

Published by Metz Press
1 Cameronians Avenue
Welgemoed, 7530
South Africa

First published in 2007
Copyright © Metz Press 2007
Copyright in text, artwork, templates © Lesley Turpin-Delport, Nicola Delport-Wepener
Commissioned photographs copyright © Metz Press

Publisher and editor	Wilsia Metz
Photographer	Ivan Naudé
Design and lay-out	Lindie Metz
Production assistant	Rowina Keiller
Reproduction	Color/Fuzion, Greenpoint
Printed and bound in China by Imago	
ISBN	978-1-919992-81-5

content

Introduction

Just stitch is a culmination of ten years of teaching in many countries, and absorbing the storehouse of inspiration. The input and enthusiasm of embroiderers and the many different embroidery techniques that one rediscovers on a journey of this kind are portrayed in the book. The beautiful photomontages of scenery, flora and fauna and embroidery examples are included to fire your imagination. It is a visual guide to where you can find inspiration.

The theme is fauna and flora, and the central application the use of an abundance of hand-dyed and textured fibres. This wealth of textures has been simplified by beginning with one single stitch, namely couching. Embedded in the many projects in the book are glorious techniques, finally moving into the third dimension. The projects cater for different skills and levels of expertise and offer a wide spectrum of choice for all needlecrafters.

The beginning of *Just stitch* deals with basic necessities, followed by a most useful chapter on techniques with new dimensions and ideas. These include working with textured threads, ribbon work focusing on organza and taffeta, the manipulation of wool and felt, appliqué techniques (ideal for quilters), a dash of beading, doing photo transfers, working with net (tulle), elevated shapes including stumpwork (wired work) and barbola (unwired elevated shapes). This section will help you understand and implement mixed-media embroidery. To introduce the concept of Just stitch there is a photograph of an agapanthus bloom which inspired a painting. The painting is used in an application to illustrate scale and shading, and in a project as a textured interpretation of *Agapanthus africanus,* ideal for a cushion or quilt block, while the more complex interpretation of the agapanthus plant, in the third dimension, is perfect for a framed picture.

Twelve colours are represented and each colour break offers you two projects within the spectrum – one simple and another more adventurous. Scattered between the colours are spreads of inspiration within the individual colour range. We have given in-depth descriptions for certain projects and techniques while other images are there for you to interpret in whichever technique, colour and thread grab the imagination.

We conclude the book with a stitch gallery for ease of reference, and a bumper section of templates so you can start working on your own creative projects with textured threads immediately.

Have a fabulous time enjoying mixed-media embroidery with a wide variety of threads and techniques.

Just stitch!

Les and Nikki

Right: Symphony of flowers

The sewing basket

Needles and necessities

A box of crayons, pots of paint, threads, cottons and silks all create embroidery notions. When you feel like a little fancy work, select exciting fabric and choose the right needle and thread to match. These are part of the little pleasures of life that give so much enjoyment.

Embroidery is a creative process, so free your imagination and experiment with threads to express your ideas.

Threads

STRANDED COTTON (FLOSS)

A shiny six-strand thread that can be split into any number of threads up to six according to the thickness of the fabric, the desired effect and the embroiderer's special know-how. It is the best choice for cross stitch, padded and unpadded satin stitch and crewel embroidery.

PERLÉ COTTON

Shiny, twisted thread, ideal for beginners: it does not come untwisted and thus ensures uniform stitches. Excellent results on pure cotton, all linen and even weave fabrics.

SOFT COTTON (TAPESTRY COTTON)

Thick, matt thread, 100% cotton is soft and flexible and very easy to use on coarse or basket-weave canvases.

COTTON A BRODER/FLOWER THREAD

Fine, matt cotton thread.

TAPESTRY WOOL

Suitable for embroidery on softly textured, loosely woven material.

CREWEL WOOL

Mothproof, 100% pure virgin wool, soft and fine, ideal for delicate wool work.

CRAZY WOOLS

This range offers the embroidery enthusiast limitless scope. Most craft and wool shops offer an exquisite range of fringed, feathered, dyed, knotted and tangled combinations of exotic wool. Pure wool, such as lamb's wool, angora, mohair and pure silk, is also an option. Wool can be manipulated into a design with couching or simply knitted into a shape and hand embroidered onto the background.

YARN

Mercerized thread which is part synthetic and part natural fibre (more or less equivalent to no 12 perlé).

TEXTURED THREADS

A selection of threads that suggest a raised dimension: chenille (velvet pile), bouclé (knotted pile), round rayon cord and flat knitted rayon ribbon

SPACE-DYED AND VARIEGATED THREADS

Talented designers world wide have created a vast range of hand-dyed, variegated threads which are marvellous for free style embroidery.

QUILTING THREADS

Commercial quilting threads are now available in all colours, but if you can't find any, use a pure cotton thread (no 30) and run it through beeswax to prevent it from tangling.

UNUSUAL THREADS

Additional thread types which are exciting when mixed to create different textures and colour combinations, include pure silk, rayon, viscose, linen and metallic thread.

MACHINE THREADS

Machine threads are ideal for satin stitch around machine appliqué. These threads are also stronger when used as tacking thread.

Rayon machine threads are suitable for the basic stitching for the Barbola technique. They also offer a gentle sheen to the final shape.

Ribbons

PURE SILK

Pure silk ribbon is available in several widths from 2-13 mm. It is so soft that it can be pulled through the background fabric just like embroidery floss.

RAW SILK

Raw silk ribbon tape can be manipulated onto background fabric and pulled through, if the fabric is not too fine.

ORGANZA AND RAYON

Organza ribbon is also available in a range of widths and is used in the same way as pure silk. Use organzawhen a transparent or very delicate effect is required.

SATIN RIBBON

Satin ribbon is best manipulated off the background fabric. Construct leaves and flowers as free-form shapes and then work them onto the background using invisible stitches.

Embroidery fabrics

All fabrics can be used for embroidery, but the following are highly recommended:

FINE AND MEDIUM FABRICS

Pure linen, pure cotton, linen-cotton mixture

COARSE LINEN AND EVEN WEAVE (14 COUNT)

These are more open fabrics to make counting threads and stitches easier.

EXOTIC FABRICS

These include moiré taffeta, pure silk, raw silk, velvet, fine corduroy and antique handkerchiefs, or netting (fine tulle) used for double-sided images on a very delicate base.

TAPESTRY FABRIC

This is ideal for handbags, embellished with textured threads and beads to enhance selected motifs.

FOUNDATION FABRIC

This is used to give the work body and to hide the beginnings and endings of threads. Muslin is an extremely loose weave while cotton voile has a tighter warp and weft.

FELT

The thickness and quality of felt vary. Pure wool is suitable for felt stems and a foundation to stitch on as it is thick and durable. Hand-dyed colours in muted shades are available. Thinner felts allow for more control when layering the felt under stumpwork shapes for a more padded effect.

Needles

Use the right needle for the intended stitching to ensure the best possible results.

- Crewel needles for fine embroidery. Sharp tip, small eye.
- Chenille needles for textured threads, candlewicking and silk ribbon embroidery. Sharp tip, long eye.
- Tapestry needles for woollen embroidery. Blunt tip, long eye.
- Straw (sharps or milliners) needles for specialist stitches such as bullion and cast-on buttonhole. Very small eye, long shaft.
- Between needles for quilting. Small eye, very short shaft. This is an ideal needle for barbola as it is thin, fine and short.
- Bead needles for beading. Small eye, long and very thin shaft.
- Felting needle. This is a sharp barbed needle for working with pure wool when making felt.
- Knitting needles.

Right: Country Feeling sampler

COUNTRY

Miscellaneous requirements

EMBROIDERY SCISSORS

The ideal pair is light with fine, pointed ends to cut thread cleanly.

PLIERS

A useful tool for the manipulation of wire in stumpwork techniques.

GLUE

You will need anti-fray glue and fast-drying transparent fabric glue. For shaping and draping liquid, mix 2 parts glue and 1 part water (apply with a paint brush).

THIMBLE

This is a must for embroidery/quilting comfort.

EMBROIDERY FRAMES (HOOPS)

Cloth stretched on an embroidery frame does not pucker. Various frames are available. They come in several diameters and can be held in the hand, fixed to a stand or to the edge of a table.

BEADS

A selection of tiny beads, pearls and bugle beads is very handy to work into your embroidery for shine and dimension.

WIRE

Wire is available in a range of gauges (the most useful gauges are 28-33). The soft flexible wire (green and white, with or without paper) from specialist needlework shops, florists, cake icing suppliers or bead shops is ideal.

NOTIONS

Washers, curtain rings, found objects, Vilene, appliqué paper and wadding are used for mixed-media techniques to add dimension.

PAINT AND INKS

Colour can be added to designs prior to stitching, while cut three-dimensional shapes in techniques such as stumpwork and barbola can be touched up with permanent markers or fabric paint.

PERMANENT MARKERS

A permanent black/colour fine-liner is often used in mixed-media designs. Always test your pen to see that it is in fact colour fast. Different nib widths are available for fine or coarse work. Ink in your outline before you begin the paintwork.

FABRIC PAINTS

A water-based, permanent paint is ideal. Try different size paint brushes: a fat stiff bristle brush will give a good stipple or drag effect; a medium size, stiff bristle brush is good for the smaller areas and a small, fine brush is needed for delicate detail. Begin by testing your paint on a small piece of scrap fabric to gain a little confidence. Use the paint very diluted to give a delicate water-colour effect. Dry paint will give a good stipple, while a creamy consistency is best for filling in. Heat seal the paintwork by ironing with a hot iron (on the wrong side).

WATER COLOUR CRAYONS

These can be used on fabric. Draw first and then lightly wet the drawn line with a soft bristle brush to achieve a water-colour effect.

PHOTO TRANSFERS

A naked canvas or blank paper is often daunting to a prospective artist. An easy way to accomplish a professional finish is to colour your cloth with a photocopy transfer and then embroider the finer details (see page 16).

Destinations

Creative embroidery has many destinations.

THE LINEN CUPBOARD

Fill your linen cupboard with functional items embellished with exquisite embroidery.

Dining room and kitchen Table cloths, dinner napkins (serviettes), dinner mats, tea towels, aprons, oven mitts, pot holders, tray cloths, tea cosy and a net (cake and meat covers).

Bedroom linen Top sheets, pillow cases, duvet covers, quilts, hangers and tissue box covers.

Bathroom Bath sheets, guest hand towels, laundry bag and cosmetic bag.

Living spaces Lampshades, scatter cushions, throws, curtains, pictures, picture frames, embroidered boxes and fire screen.

THE WARDROBE

Garments have been embellished from Tutankhamen's time to the present. Certain decades truly enjoyed the full potential of decorating their robes. To go through the history of costume and finery through the centuries would involve a couple of books so to whet your appetite we will just touch on a few ideas. As you meander through the colour spectrum, imagine the inspiration for the artists of the time when they depicted the glorious clothes of the different centuries … Renaissance, Baroque, Rococo, Neo-classicism, Impressionism …

Just stitch offers techniques which are ideal for 21st Century application yet the roots of inspiration arefrom the eras listed below.

- Italian renaissance: Trapunto, casal guidi and corded quilting
- Elizabethan: Goldwork and stumpwork
- Jacobean: Crewel work
- Victorian: Ribbon work, tucks and pleats
- Roaring 20s: Tassels, fringing, ribbon roses on cloche hats, snoods, shoes and handbags
- The year 2007: Hand and machine embroidery, beading, tucks and pleats, ribbon work and smocking are seen in abundance at gala dinners, Academy Awards and celebrity weddings. Accessories such as handbags, shoes and hair apparel are as flamboyant as ever.

New dimensions – exciting techniques

Techniques will be referred to in the project section, but for practical reasons and ease of reference the details are all covered in this section. (The photographs on this page show details from the *Garden Route Sampler*, and on the opposite page is *Clivia miniata*.)

Photo transfers

Colour your cloth with a photocopy transfer and then embroider the finer details. Ask the photocopy technician to bump up the colour of your photocopy. This will give a good colour transfer.

Work on a melamine surface or a piece of smooth cardboard. Position your fabric on this surface using masking tape to keep it in place. Place the photocopy face down over the fabric. Hold the copy in position with a strip of masking tape on one side. Dampen the rag with thinners and using a firm, circular motion work into the back of the photocopy with the rag. Now take the soup spoon and repeat the circular rubbing, "spooning" the toner from the photocopy into the fabric with the back of the spoon.

Check your progress by gently lifting the photocopy to see if all the toner has penetrated the fabric. Once you are happy with your transfer, iron the design from the back to heat-seal it. Accentuate the important areas with free-style embroidery.

Tips for successful photo transfers

- Choose a clear picture with good contrasts
- Do not overload your rag with thinners. This can cause the toner to bleed into the background fabric.
- Stay small. Too large a design is not a good idea.

* You may copy images from this book for personal use, but not for commercial use or resale.

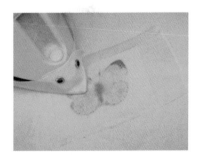

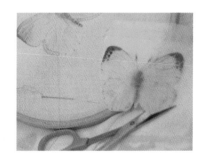

Preparation of background fabric

When working with textured threads, ribbon and new dimensions, the preparation of the background fabric is important.

If the design is not pre-printed (silk-screened onto the background), lightly sketch the design onto the fabric with an HB pencil or dressmaker's carbon. Using a light-box or a window, place the sketch chosen behind the top fabric and transfer the image onto the fabric. (See Templates pages 141-160 or order silk screens from Les Designs – contact details on page 133.)

Wet and iron your muslin (foundation fabric) before placing it behind the top fabric. Ensure that the warp and weft of the muslin and the top fabric match (in other words that the greatest stretch is in the same direction) and baste (tack) together. The muslin gives body and a foundation for beginning and ending neatly.

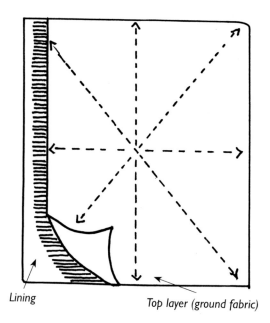

Lining

Top layer (ground fabric)

Above: Autumn-leaf vagrant. Embroidered silk photo transfer

Working with textured threads

It's so simple – just couch!

Textured (creative) threads offer the embroidery enthusiast an opportunity to experiment with the tactile quality of these threads, to enjoy the third dimension and, in many instances, to speed up the embroidery process.

Certain textured threads can be pulled through the background fabric and couched in position (rayon and organza depending on the width of the thread and the weave of the fabric). Use the chenille needle and wiggle it in the fabric to help the threads pass easily through the fabric to avoid damaging the fibres.

Other textured threads with knots or high pile (bouclé and chenille) are best worked on top of the fabric. Simply lay the textured thread down and secure the tail with a couple of holding stitches in a single strand of matching floss or fine yarn. Once the tail has been secured, proceed with **couching** (see illustration right). End with a couple of strong holding stitches.

Couching

This technique can be used in linear work or as a solid filling. Threads are laid down on the surface of the fabric and held in place with another thread. Any type of thread can be couched. Contrast colours can be used and many different holding stitches are suitable, including cross stitch, herringbone, straight stitch, fly stitch and detached chain. When couching in a circle, try to create a rhythm with the holding stitches by controlling the pattern made by the stitches. Or Nué is a wonderful 17th century antique technique where a single strand of thread is couched over a cord in concentrated areas of different colours to create the illusion of the pattern required. Using hand-dyed stranded cotton for this can be very effective.

Floss or yarn (mercerised part synthetic fibre) is an ideal couching thread. It is stronger than stranded cotton and is colour fast.

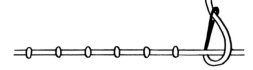

CHENILLE

Pluck the velvet fluff from the cotton core.

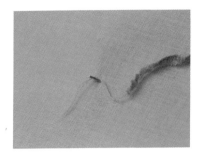

Always work from the front of the design to the back.

Couch the chenille with a matching yarn.

To anchor chenille pluck the velvet fluff from the cotton core (3 cm in length). Thread the cotton core into a large chenille needle (no18) and push it into the background from the front of the design. Secure the cotton tail at the back of the work with matching floss or yarn in anticipation of couching the chenille thread in place.

To anchor round rayon, gently pull the rayon thread from the cotton core (3 cm in length). Thread the cotton core into a large chenille needle (no 18) and push it into the background from the front of the design. Now thread the fine rayon into the background and use this to secure the cotton tail at the back of the work. Proceed with couching on top of the fabric.

ROUND RAYON CORD

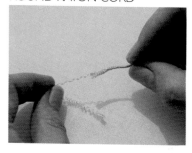

Gently pull the rayon thread from the cotton core without breaking the rayon.

Thread into a large chenille needle (no 18) and plunge the cotton core from the front to the back and secure in the muslin fabric.

Take the rayon through to the back and cover the cotton core with overcast stitches.

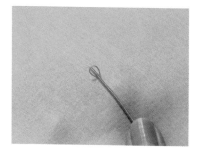

Take matching yarn and make small, regular stitches over the cord

The holding stitch can also be *invisible*.

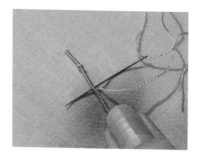

Perforate the cord through the centre and plunge immediately back into the fabric. Make stitches about 3 mm apart and pull down firmly on the thread.

Couching can also be invisible. Secure the cords by slip hemming them in place by pushing the thread through the belly of the cord using a matching thread. Push the needle into the background immediately so the connecting stitches are invisible.

KNITTED (FLAT) RAYON CORD

Use no 18 chenille needle and work from the front to the back.

Select matching yarn and either couch over the cord …

… or through the belly of the cord to hold in place. This type of cord can also be ruched.

With crazy wools (fringed wool, knotted wool, mohair, tangled wool combinations etc.) knitting the shape is also an option. Large wooden needles are perfect for knitting up fringed wools. The shape can be attached to the background and the fringe trimmed to form a tufted effect.

Bouclé is handled in the same manner as the crazy wools.

FRINGED/FEATHERED WOOL

Fringed/feathered wool is perfect couched and manipulated to shade as the colour changes. It's easy to work

with threaded into a no 18 chenille needle (see owlet page 104). Secure fringed/feathered wool from the front

to the back. Couch the upper edge in matching yarn and, when layering, start at the base and work upwards.

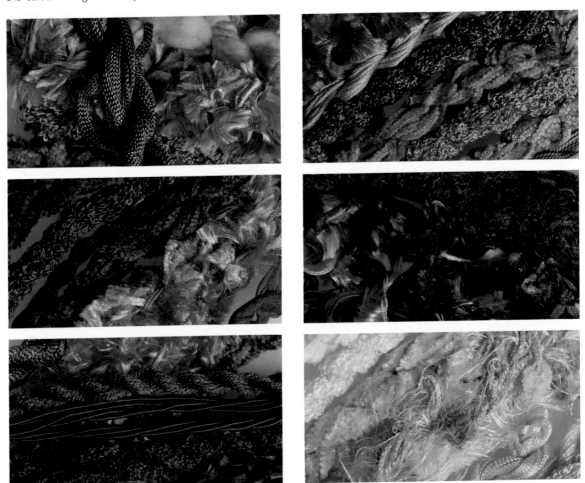

Scale and shading

These concepts are best explained by sharing with you our agapanthus story.

The beautiful agapanthus (*Agapanthus africanus*) flowers in mid December. It is indigenous to the Southern Cape region of South Africa, popularly known as the Garden Route. The plant is made up of a cluster of leaves, large and small stems, and the flower head (the bloom). The head of the agapanthus has a number of components: buds, half open buds, the full bloom and spent flowers. The basic trumpet has six petals, five to six stamens, a pistil and a slim stem which supports the trumpet. The calyx is sometimes visible. A glorious display of multiple blooms inspired a painting. The painting (photocopied and transferred to fabric) in turn was the inspiration for creative needlework.

and sturdy, durable textured threads. The agapanthus interpretation of *Agapanthus africanus* on page 85 is ideal for a scatter cushion as the choice of texture and stitches makes the cushion tactile and washable.

Size

Choose the size (scale) of the design to suit your item. Begin with basic appliqué (see page 23), outlined in buttonhole stitch. The images that suit appliqué are the leaves, some of the buds and trumpets. Select fabric such as hand-dyed cotton, ombre taffeta or silk that would do justice to the plant. Finish the basic appliqué and then START with the main stem and small stalks. The small stalks (slim

We noticed the *colour* and *composition* in each trumpet of the bloom which inspired much of the creative work you see here. We will take you on a journey of discovering the different techniques that will work for many different needle crafters.

These techniques are similar to, yet different from the agapanthus interpretation on page 85.

When you embark on a creative embroidery journey, the choice of fabric, thread and medium will be dictated by the item you are making. An embroidered panel for a quilt, for example, should be embellished with washable

stem) can be done in shades of evergreen and olive in stem stitch.

Shading

To enhance the texture of the appliquéd leaves, work into the central vein with light and dark tones of lime and evergreen bouclé and chenille. Choose a light source and maintain the vibe throughout.

Delineate the petal divisions of the dark blue trumpet in a toning floss (single strand). The light blue trumpet petal division can be delineated in a lilac or blue floss in split stitch. The outline of the light blue trumpet is accentuated with a couched deep blue bouclé.

The main stem is couched down the centre of the olive green knitted, rayon cord, with matching yarn, in stem stitch. Shade in lime green for a highlight and evergreen for a lowlight.

Different applications

Recommended for quilts at this stage: stitch the receding flowers in single strand, chain stitch embroidery with light and dark blue floss. Small buds are couched in light and dark blue bouclé. Slightly larger buds are couched in blue chenille. The two dominant open blooms in the centre could be three or five-spoke picot in variegated perlé. Pistils and stamens could be extended French knots in light blue floss, single strand, capped with a fine charcoal bullion. The recommended choice of stitches suits the fact that the quilt will need to be used and laundered.

For framed pictures you can be more adventurous. The dominant flowers at the front of the bloom can be worked in 6 mm wide azure blue *organza ribbon*. As the organza is transparent, it would be a good idea to either embroider the stripe of the petal or to sketch it in blue pen and then to stitch with the organza ribbon. Make six stab stitch petals for the trumpet shape. Decorate the centre with an artificial pistil and stamens. Surround these with two small bullions in light blue floss. Soft withered leaves can be stab stitched in olive green 15 mm organza ribbon. These leaves can be embellished with stem stitch in olive green yarn.

Part of the bloom can be offset as one would see it displayed in a botanical painting. This could be a wire-edged taffeta specimen – a wonderful completely three-dimensional bloom constructed by making and assembling a number of three-dimensional trumpets (see page 25 for instructions).

The two dominant blooms work beautifully in *barbola* (see page 26). An idea unique to Les Designs, would be to work the three-dimensional petals over an organza stab stitch to elevate the shape instead of using draping and shaping liquid. The suggestion for stamens and pistil would be drizzle stitch, with or without a bead at the tip (see Agapanthus project page 85).

Some agapanthus varieties are white. Follow the suggestions above, change the blue ribbons and threads to white and use a softly coloured background to show off the white blooms. The exquisite orange multi-trumpeted *Clivia miniata* (see page 15), also indigenous to the region, can be interpreted using these ideas.

Appliqué

Use hand-dyed cotton, silk or taffeta for appliqué images to enhance your embroidery.

Materials required

Appliqué paper or iron-on Vilene
Hand-dyed cotton, silk or taffeta
Sharp scissors
Matching floss
Needle
Iron, pencil and tacking thread

Trace the image onto appliqué paper or iron-on Vilene, rough side facing upwards, with a soft pencil. Cut out the shape on the outline and iron the cut-out, rough side down, onto the wrong side of the fabric.

If you use appliqué paper, cut out the paper-backed fabric on the outline. Peel off the paper, position the delicate cotton, silk or taffeta shape on the background fabric and iron in place.

If you use iron-on Vilene, tack the Vilene-backed shape into position on the background or lightly glue it down with stationery glue.

Buttonhole the raw edges in matching floss, single strand. The shapes are now ready for embellishment with fine embroidery details.

Brenton Blue taffeta appliqué detail

Brenton Blue butterfly taffeta series

The cosmos design shows hand appliqué with buttonhole and embroidered embellishment.

Appliqué: Wire-edged

Make an agapanthus specimen

Use wire-edged appliqué to make three-dimensional blooms, wings and other objects to enhance your embroidery. Here we take you through the steps to make a wire-edged agapanthus bloom with taffeta ribbon. Use appliqué paper and gauge 28 wire.

Materials required
Appliqué paper
Taffeta ribbon
Iron
Matching stranded cotton
Sharp scissors
Gauge 28 wire
No 8/9 quilting needle
Anti-fray glue
5/6 artificial stamens
4 mm round blue bead
Clear-drying fabric glue
Green yarn/floss

1 Use the template on page 150 and trace the petals (6) onto appliqué paper. Cut out the shapes. Follow the cut out shapes with the wire, leaving a 2 cm tail at the beginning and end of the shape. These tails will be used in assembling the trumpet on completion of all six petals.

2 Iron the appliqué paper cut out onto one half of the taffeta ribbon. Gently peel the appliqué paper off the ribbon and be sure the adhesive web remains on the ribbon. Lay the wire around the adhesive web image. Fold over the other half of the ribbon so that it covers the wire which surrounds the web (the web is almost invisible, but holds the 2 layers of ribbon in place once ironed).

3 Select matching stranded cotton and whip the wire evenly around the shape, leaving a tail of at least 6 cm when beginning and ending. Delineate the vein using stem stitch which creates a perfect back stitch on the underside. Use an ear bud to apply anti-fray glue around the outside of the whipped petal shape. Leave the fluid to dry overnight. Cut very carefully around the shape and as close to the stitching as possible, keeping anti-fray glue handy should you cut a stitch.

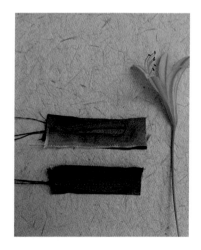

4 Cut one wire away from the base of each petal. Hold all six petals together and select one of the petal wires to wrap around the rest of the wire bundle. Wrap tightly.

5 Push the stamens into the hole of the bead. Add a dash of fabric glue to hold them in place. Glue the bead with its stamens inside the base of the 6 petals. For extra strength use the dangling threads to secure the bead and end off each thread at the base of the petals as securely as possible. If necessary, work these threads up the trumpet shape of the petal to secure the configuration.

6 Select a green yarn/floss and attach with a backstitch at the base of the trumpet. Run a layer of clear-drying fabric glue along the length of the wire then wrap the yar/floss tightly around the wires, wiping away any excess glue.

A number of these trumpets can be assembled to create a life-size agapanthus head. Alternatively it can be connected to the background as a specimen. An orange three-dimensional clivia trumpet could be made using the same technique.

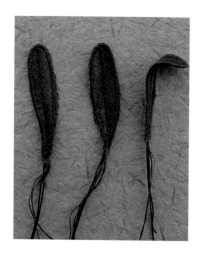

Barbola

Unwired stumpwork: make a barbola agapanthus trumpet

Barbola originated in Ancient Tibet and is a form of embroidery art that combines embroidery and embossment. In recent years gifted embroidery folk have adapted this ancient Tibetan technique and created non-wired, hand embroidered images, shaped and stiffened with glue instead of paper models.

The needle crafter can interpret Barbola in a very fine thread such as rayon machine thread or fine pure silk. It is also effective in a bolder technique using embroidery thread or crewel wool.

Materials required
HB pencil
Swiss batiste or very fine cotton
Embroidery hoop
Embroidery threads: pearl, teal, light blue, dark brown stranded cotton/floss or silk rayon for a very fine effect
Shaping and draping fluid
Ear bud
Sharp scissors
No 9/10 between needle, beading needle
Permanent marker or fabric paint
Small bronze, black or yellow beads
Tweezers
Anti-fray glue

1   Use the template on page 150 and trace the petals (6) onto the fabric and place into a hoop (embroidery ring). Secure the thread by seeding into the shape and work towards the outline of the image. Outline the shape first in fine backstitch. Buttonhole the outer edge with long and short stitches very closely aligned (the stitches need to be fine and dense). Once around the shape, take your thread into the centre, ending with a few back stitches.

2   Select the colours for the shading of the shape. Work long and short split stitch using single-strand embroidery thread, grading the colour from teal at the tip of the petal moving towards a light blue at the base with a vibrant blue stripe in the centre. Start in the centre towards the tip of the petal and make approximately 2 to 3 split stitches to meet the buttonhole pearl edge at the tip of the petal. Stab down and up in 2 separate movements, the first stab stitch downwards must be quite small, the upward stitch that splits the thread must be at least three quarters up the back of the stab stitch for a perfect double-sided petal. Continue to work in a horizontal rhythm across the petal from centre to the left, back to centre and then to the right, staggering the base

stitches as you fill the shape. When changing colour be sure to continue the horizontal rhythm of the split stitch and maintain the staggered base. This will help with contouring the shape. In order for the petal to be successful the front and the back of the petal must be the same.

3   Complete all six petals, apply shaping and draping fluid with a cotton ear bud to the fine background fabric just touching the pearl edge of the buttonhole and allow to dry overnight.

4   With very sharp scissors cut out the petals being extremely careful not to cut the stitches. Keep your anti-fray handy in case of any accidents. Colour in the edge of the petal with a matching permanent marker or fabric paint to camouflage any filaments of fabric that may be exposed. Mix fabric stiffener, 2 parts glue to 1 part water, in a small pill bottle. With a fine soft bristle brush apply the mixture to the underside of the petal, allow five minutes drying time and then

shape petals (use tweezers to aid the shaping of the curled back petal tips). Support the shape on a small sponge using pins if necessary to maintain the shape. Allow 24 hours drying time. Wash the brush in warm water once finished.

5   Create the bloom by carefully slip-hemming each petal to its neighbour. If the curled petals have changed once the trumpet is complete, reapply more fluid and shape again. Connect the base of the trumpet to the background fabric with matching thread using a few very strong back stitches.

6   With single-strand, dark brown floss create stamens by pushing a bead needle through the background fabric into the trumpet base and end with a petite bronze/black or yellow bead onto the background or petal surface. Alternatively use artificial stamens, push them into the base of the trumpet and connect with invisible stitches. (See wired-edged appliqué page 24, for a bead option page 85.)

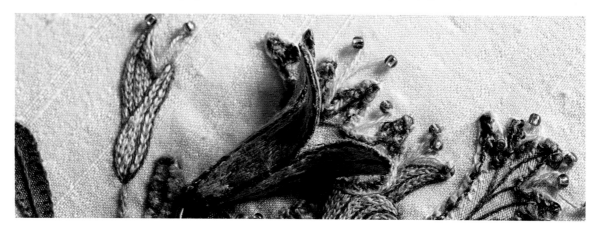

Stumpwork-inspired techniques

Elevated shapes

Elevated shapes are ideal for wings, petals or leaves. Stumpwork shapes can be wired, or done without wire. The advantage of wiring the embroidery is the added dimension of being able to shape, bend and position the images once they have been embroidered. The soft flexible gauge 28 wire from specialist needlework shops, florists, cake-icing outlets or bead shops is ideal.

Two different dimentional techniques are seen here: needlelace on wire and taffeta with a butonholed wire edge.

Wire on pure silk, organza or taffeta

This option works best where the beauty of the background fabric peeps through the covered wire and the fine embellishing stitches. The background fabric is not covered completely, for example with butterfly or dragonfly wings.

Materials required
Pure silk, organza or taffeta
Embroidery hoop
Tacking thread
Embroidery thread
Gauge 28 wire
No 9/10 between needles
Sharp scissors

1   Place the fabric in a hoop and tighten. Trace the shapes onto the fabric. Using a matching thread baste the wire to the fabric around the image, leaving two tails of wire at the base of the shape. Stitch the wire to the fabric by buttonholing around the wire in single-strand matching or contrasting thread (depending on design).

2   Decorate the shape with details using the fine between needle to avoid damaging the fabric. The underside should be as good as the top side so choose stitches which will enhance the work, such as satin stitch, couching, stab stitch, feather stitch and stem stitch (see agapanthus specimen page 85).

3   Use sharp scissors to cut out the shape close to the edge but be careful not to cut the stitches or tails. Secure the shapes by pushing the wire tails and thread through the background fabric. Bend the wire back against the fabric and secure with the embroidery thread tails. Always assemble the dimensional shapes last.

Hint: This technique can be double-sided, especially if you would like two-tone petals.

Wire worked on background with satin stitch fill

Elevated shapes

This method is suitable for petals, leaves, wings and fins. The image is satin stitched and buttonholed and includes a piece of wire on a base of fabric, held taut in an embroidery hoop.

Materials required
Background fabric
Embroidery hoop
Tacking thread
Embroidery thread: matching stranded cotton/floss or silk rayon
Gauge 28 wire
9/10 crewel needle
Sharp scissors

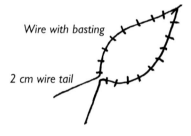

Wire with basting

2 cm wire tail

Hint: If available use the same colour wire and fabric as your choice of embroidery thread

1   Place the fabric in a hoop and tighten. Trace the shapes onto the fabric. Baste or couch a piece of covered wire over the shape leaving a short wire tail.

2   The wire can be covered with buttonhole or whipped very closely with a matching colour or contrast thread in single or two strands. Leave a tail at the beginning and end to be used later to attach the shape to the background fabric.

3   Fill the inside of the wired shape with long and short satin stitch, leaving a 5 cm tail at the beginning. Use a single-strand fine thread, working very neatly so that both the front and the back of the work are perfect. End with a tail.

4   Once the images are complete, use a very fine, sharp pair of scissors to cut away the excess background fabric. Be careful not to cut your embroidery threads. Some needle crafters protect the outer stitching with anti-fray glue.

5   Embellish the individual shapes such as petals with extended French knots for stamens or wings with simple stab stitch for veins. This can be done on individual shapes, or on completion of the flower shape, butterfly wing or petal, once the shapes have been attached to the background fabric.

Needle-lace on wire (hand held)

Elevated shapes

This technique resembles miniature crochet. It is only wire and thread and does not have a base fabric.

Materials required
Embroidery thread: stranded cotton yarn or perlé
Gauge 28 wire
No 22 chenille needle
Design or template

1 Shaping the wire: Position the wire over the traced design. Leaving a small tail which can be pushed through the fabric on completion, shape the wire to match the basic image and leave a small tail at the end, matching the beginning tail. Perlé or yarn is easy to manage and therefore the best choice of thread for this technique as the wire is hand-held.

2 Use a chenille needle and buttonhole around the wire, leaving a tail of thread for securing the shape to the background on completion. Keep the 'pearl' side of the buttonhole on the inside of the shape. Work into these loops with semi-detached buttonhole fillers, thus completing the shape. End with a tail which can be used to secure the wire at the back of the work.

Hint: Another option would be to use a vertical spider's web after the first round of buttonhole instead of semi-detached buttonhole – ideal for a butterfly's wing as illustrated below.

Tendrils

Elevated shapes

This technique can also be used for attached or detached tendrils. Use this technique for butterflies' legs and feelers and the antennae of crabs.

Materials required
Embroidery thread: stranded cotton or perlé
Gauge 28 wire
No 7/8 crewel needle
Pliers (optional)
Toothpick

Attached tendrils: Make a knot 2 cm along the wire, leaving a thread tail. Buttonhole around the wire for about 6 cm, leaving a thread tail at each end for securing the shape to the background on completion. End with a knot and a thread tail which can be used to secure the wire at the back of the work. Wrap the thread-covered wire around a toothpick then gently slip the coiled wire off the toothpick. Push each wire end into the back-

ground fabric and secure with the thread tails. Assemble the tendrils when all the other embroidery is complete.

Detached tendrils: Cut a 10 cm length of wire and bend the end into a small loop. Take the embroidery thread through the loop leaving a tail and make three buttonhole stitches into the top of the loop. Use a pair of pliers and squeeze the loop tightly together.

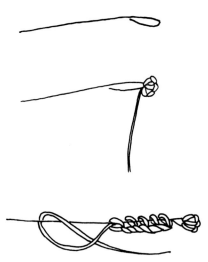

Continue buttonholing or wrapping down the shaft of the wire, losing the tail under the wraps or stitches. Stop 1 cm short of the end. Make a knot and leave a tail. Wrap the thread-covered wire around a toothpick and then gently push the coils off the toothpick, ready for assembly onto the background fabric.

Wrapping found objects

Buttonhole curtain rings or washers in the same manner as the tendril wire and be sure to leave securing tails on both ends.

Needlelace with wire on background support

Elevated shapes

The shape (petal, wing or leaf) is stitched over a piece of wire on a base of fabric, held taut in an embroidery hoop.

Materials required
Background fabric
Embroidery hoop
Embroidery thread: stranded cotton or perlé (yarn)
Gauge 28 wire
No 22 chenille needle
Sharp scissors

1   Place the fabric in a hoop and tighten. Trace the shapes onto the fabric. Baste or couch a piece of covered wire along the shape outline.

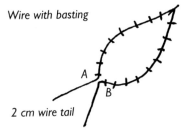

Wire with basting

2 cm wire tail

2   Leaving a tail of about 5 cm, begin buttonhole at A and work around the shape ending at B. Skim past the fabric, working only on the wire and end with a tail of thread and keep the buttonhole loops on the inside.

3   Continue in semi-detached buttonhole until the shape is filled. Bring the thread down through the image ending it off at the base.

4   Remove carefully from the background fabric by snipping the basting threads at the back of the work. Do not cut the embroidery threads off. These threads will be used to attach the petals on completion of all stitching.

Hint: To attach a wired shape to the background, make a hole in the fabric with a large needle and insert the wire through the hole. Bend the tails of the shape backwards so they lie flat against the background fabric. Sew the thread tails through the background fabric to secure.

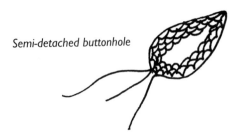

Semi-detached buttonhole

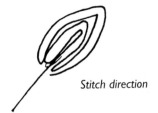

Stitch direction

Folded wired shapes

Elevated shapes

This technique works particularly well for birds' feathers, oak leaves and fig leaves.

Materials required
Gauge 28-33 wire
Variegated green perlé
Needles
Sharp scissors
Pliers (optional)

1 Make a knot on the wire, leaving a thread tail that will be used to attach the shape on completion. Buttonhole along the wire for about 6 cm. Use variegated green perlé or yarn as this is easier to needle-lace. Cast on and off, working in semi-detached buttonhole to create five scallops as you work. The size of the scallops will be determined by the shape you are creating.

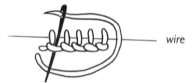

wire

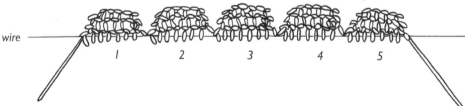

wire   I   2   3   4   5

2 Once the scallops are complete, bend the wire in half and join with overcast stitch down the middle.

3 Put the shape aside until all the embroidery is complete. To assemble, push the wire through the background fabric, bend the wire back on itself and then secure with the dangling threads.

Dimensional picot petals

Elevated shapes

Ideal for free-standing three-dimensional items such as the gerbera flowers (see project on page 61).

Materials required
Gauge 28-33 wire
Variegated red perlé
No 22 tapestry needle
Sharp scissors
Pliers

1   Cut the wire into suitable lengths for these petals. Bend each wire in half around your finger, measure 3 cm from the bottom of the wire and twist the wire.
2   Thread up with about 90 cm variegated red perlé. Leaving a 7 cm tail to attach the petal on completion, make a knot on one of the wires above the twist.

Use a tapestry needle and weave back and forth over the wire from the base of the shape to the top. This motion is similar to a 2-spoke woven picot. Weave firmly. At the top, wrap the thread three times over the wire then lose the thread inside the petal. To hide the thread, enter at the top of the last wrap between the woven threads and wiggle the needle through the centre of all the woven threads back to the base. Be careful not to pull too hard as this will distort the weaving on the wire (see daigrams A & B, page 145.

3   You will be left with 2 tails for connecting the petal. If holding the wire is difficult connect the wire shape to a fabric base with tacking stitches, weave the wire and cut away the holding stitches on completion (see page 145).

Trapunto quilting

This is also called high-relief quilting – an attractive form of quilting where selected areas of an embroidered design are padded to give a raised effect. The trapunto is done once the outline embroidery is complete.

Embroidery thread for backstitch

Wadding

Toothpick or sharp bodkin

1   Prepare for trapunto quilting by sewing the embroidered fabric and the muslin backing together around the selected area. At the back of your design pry the weave of the muslin apart with a toothpick or sharp bodkin. Push small amounts of wadding into the area to be padded, using a needle.

2   Close the back by pushing the warp and weft (weave) together with the toothpick or bodkin.

The vase was enhanced with trapunto for added dimension

Blue Manna crab with trapunto under the shell

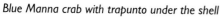

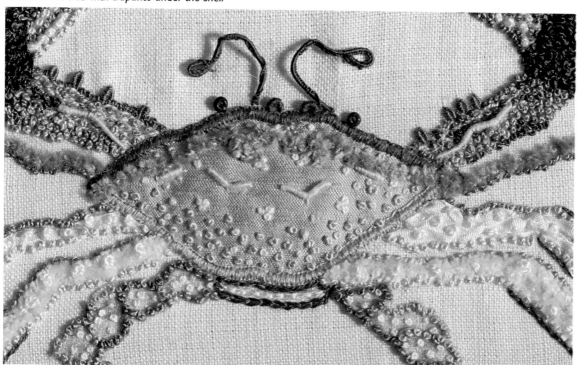

Felt

Make a three-dimensional pomegranate

Adjectives that spring to mind when we think of the intrinsic value of felt are woolly, hand-made, tactile, furry, soft, and hairy – ideal for fauna and flora!

Felt is available in exquisite hand dyed colours and various thicknesses.

Using felt enables the needle crafter to move into the third dimension with ease as felt has substance and does not fray. In *Just stitch* we use felt as a base for padded satin stitch or split stitch which elevates the shape. It is user friendly when creating three-dimensional fruit in particular. Here we explain its use in creating a transverse section of a pomegranate, where each segment is embellished with stitching, connected and assembled to create the final fruit. Cherries and berries can be constructed in the same way!

Materials required
Hand-dyed felt: red, cream/beige
Embroidery thread in various shades of red, pink, apricot, ochre – stranded cotton (floss) and perlé
Organza ribbon, 6 mm (cinnamon and red)
Red beads, small and medium
No 22 chenille and no 7/8 long straw needle
Sharp scissors
Polyester wadding

1　Trace the template on 155 onto tracing paper and use it to cut three segments of the outer skin in hand dyed red felt. Back stitch the three shapes together starting from the base to the spent end of the fruit. This allows you to hold the image and create the shading.

2　Cover the shape in split stitch, shading it at the same time. Choose a selection of yarn or embroidery threads, ranging from brown at the base, and changing colours in the following order: shades of red, pink, mustard ochre, apricot ending with a rusty red at the top. Keep the stitches short and regular. Finish the top edge of the fruit with five detached picot stitches in dark red yarn or floss.

3　Cut out the open face shape in cream/beige felt (or hand painted fabric) to form the transverse section of the pomegranate. Embroider this piece with cinnamon (pith) and red organza ribbon in small randomly scattered stab stitches. Add small red beads to the centre of the red organza stab stitch (pips). Scatter a combination of variegated red cast-on buttonhole in perlé or floss in between the organza ribbon. Attach bigger red beads between the pairs of cast-on buttonhole. Tiny stamens are extended French knots in single-strand brown floss at the tip of the fruit.

4　With right sides together, back stitch the transverse section to the outer skin, leaving a small opening at the base. Trim and clip seams and turn through. Push polyester wadding into the cavity and slip hem the opening closed. Extra subtle shading can be added to the basic pomegranate shape to camouflage any joins.

Left: A pomegranate showing the colour variations on the outer skin and the inspiration from the original fruit.
On the opposite page the completed transverse section shows clever placement of the beads to resemble the fruit.

Exposed felt images

Make a free-standing gerbera flower

Consisting mostly of felt shapes, several three-dimensional techniques are used in a unique combination to construct this striking free-standing gerbera.

Materials required
Hand-dyed felt: red, green
Embroidery threads, various stranded cotton, perlé and yarn
Hand-dyed cotton, dupion silk
Gauge 28 and 18 wire,
No 22 tapestry, no 5/6 straw and no 7/8 crewel needles
Sharp scissors
Polyester wadding
Toothpick
Pliers (optional)

1   Make the petals and centre as described on page 61 of the projects, using red felt, cotton and dupion silk. Make nine wired picot petals as described on page 34, and cut two green felt calyxes and a stem using the template on page 144.

2   Now start with the gathered ventre. Attach the wired picot petals to the base of the embroidered centre at the gathers (leave the wire tails protruding) and use the dangling thread tails to secure. These petals must not protrude further than the petal whorls, which follow. Once they are all connected, twist the wires together in the centre to form a mini stem. Take a length of thick green florist wire (gauge 18), make a loop and hem the loop into the felt base. For extra strength, twist the fine picot petal wires (mini stem) firmly around the central stalk wire (see page 145 diagram D as well as page 34).

3   Slip hem the smallest petal whorl onto the wire, through the cut cross. Stitch this whorl to the centre base as invisibly as possible. Slip the next two whorls over the wire and connect in the same manner. Put the exotic fabric uppermost.

4   First connect the larger calyx to the back of the petal whorl with green floss (keep the stitches invisible), then the smaller calyx.

Here we used felt for the under layer of petals (whorls). The buttonhole stitching is only used on the outline to attach the other layer of fabric.

Layers of raw edge, hand-dyed felt are assembled at the base of the whorl of petals.

*Be daring (and frugal) and fill a vase with
multi-coloured gerberas for lasting colour.*

5   Make the stem. Wrap the felt stem around the wire
and stitch in a circular rhythm to attach at the calyx
only. Roll the wadding in your hands to create a
sausage and embed the green wire into it. Join the
stem seam around the wadding, making sure the
wadding is evenly distributed around the wire. Butt
the two raw edges of the felt together with invisible
stitching and insert a second green wire into the
cavity, once you have stitched about 5 cm down
the shaft. To aid the rolling and stitching motion,
use a toothpick to control the wadding and wire (if
desperate use a tiny blob of water-based glue). Cut
away any remaining wire or wadding and close the
tip.

6   Make six 2-spoke woven picot calyxes in green
variegated perle/yarn. The arrangement for these
six shapes is from the base of the stem into the
alternate small V's of the felt calyx. Make another
set of six picots filling in the alternate V's, starting
just above the pervious row. Lose all beginning and
ending threads under the picot stitches.

*A padded wire-core stem is covered with a roll of hand-dyed
green felt and delicately slip hemmed in position.*

*Once complete, complement the calyx with long 2-spoke
woven picots in shades of green yarn.*

Ribbon techniques

Stitching, applique and elevated shapes

Embroidery with soft ribbon (silk, organza, rayon) is fun and quick to do. The stitches used are the same as those used in traditional embroidery floss, but the soft ribbon gives the stitches exciting dimensions. Keep the ribbon flat as it is threaded in and out of the fabric and control the tension on the ribbon and you will be thrilled with the result. See stitch glossary on page 140 for popular ribbon stitches.

Three-dimensional strawberry with dimensional silk ribbon leaves (7 mm silk ribbon).

The underside of the Brenton Blue butterfly using hand-dyed silk ribbon as the base for embroidery embellishment.

Length of ribbon

Cut the ribbon at an angle to approximately 30 cm (12 in) in length. Too long a ribbon will fray and twist, which will not enhance your embroidery.

Threading the needle

Thread the ribbon through the eye of the needle, pull about 5 cm (2 in) through then pierce the ribbon approximately 1 cm (½ in) from the end. Pull the long end of the ribbon downwards until the ribbon locks into the eye

of the needle. This prevents the needle from unthreading while you work.

Beginning and ending

We like to work with a muslin foundation behind the background fabric. This gives the work more body and allows for a neat beginning and ending.

Start by leaving a small tail hanging at the back of your work. As you make your first stitch, pierce the tail with the needle to secure the ribbon. If you find the tail securing difficult while doing tricky combinations, make a small backstitch in the foundation fabric.

To finish off your stitch, take the ribbon through to the back and work a small backstitch into the foundation fabric through the ribbon. Be careful not to snag the embroidered ribbon in that area. Don't leave a tail which can be caught when the next thread is started.

Tips when working with ribbon

Simple embroidery stitches work best with ribbon.

- Manipulate the ribbon correctly.
- The flat face of the ribbon should be laid down smoothly, without twists.
- Keep the ribbon thread short.
- Use your left thumb to hold the ribbon flat, and only release the thumb as you complete the stitch.
- You can hold the ribbon in place, when making certain stitches, with a pin or tapestry needle.
- Make sure that the ribbon is evenly spread once you have pulled it through the base fabric.
- Do not jump from one part of your design to another, as the colour might show through the background fabric.
- To prevent puckering, you should work with a small (8 cm/3 in) embroidery ring.

- To spread the ribbon, bring the needle through the fabric, hold the ribbon flat with the left thumb and slide the needle under the ribbon, towards the exit point. This should flatten the ribbon if you have used the correct needle to allow the ribbon to pass easily through the hole created by the needle.

Clever concepts with organza ribbon

Create stamens with frayed, ruched ribbon

Ruched and frayed organza ribbon creates a wonderful illusion of stamens in the scarlet passion flower.

Materials required
Organza ribbon, 25 mm wide
Machine thread to match ribbon
Needle
Sharp scissors
Pin

1 Use ribbon three times the length of the base of the petal.
2 Run a gathering thread along one side of the ribbon until it is tightly ruched and end off securely.
3 Take another thread and securely connect the gathers to the background fabric. Cut the finished edge away from the top side of the ribbon and with a pin gently fray the warp from the weft until the bristle-like effect is achieved.

Organza ribbon wings

Make an organza butterfly

Organza ribbon makes beautifully delicate wings which can be wired or unwired. Here we show you how to make wired wings.

Materials required
Gauge 28 wire
Embroidery threads: stranded cotton (floss)
Organza ribbon, 25 mm wide
No 9/10 between needle
Sharp scissors
Anti-fray glue
Ear bud
Appliqué paper
Iron

1 Trace the wings (4) onto appliqué paper (templates for butterfly wings on page 147) and cut out the shapes. Follow the cut out shapes with the wire, leaving a 2 cm tail of wire at the beginning and end of the shape. These tails will be used when assembling the butterfly on completion of the wings.

This is an organza interpretation of the Brenton Blue butterfly with the brown underside showing.

2 Iron the appliqué paper cut-out onto one side of the organza ribbon. Gently peel the appliqué paper off the ribbon ensuring that the adhesive web remains on the ribbon. Lay the wire around the adhesive web image. Place another length of organza ribbon over the first ribbon so that it covers the wire which surrounds the adhesive web (the web is almost invisible but it holds the two layers of ribbon in place once ironed. Place a handkerchief, brown paper or soft piece of fabric over the ribbon and iron to fuse the two layers of ribbon.

3 Select matching stranded cotton and whip the wire evenly around the shape, leaving a tail of at least 6 cm when beginning and ending. Delineate the vein using stab stitch which creates a perfect back stitch on the underside. Apply anti-fray fluid with an ear bud along the outside of the whipped wing shape. Leave the fluid to dry overnight. Cut very carefully around the shape and as close to the stitching as possible. Be sure to have anti-fray glue handy should you cut a stitch. Push the wires through the background fabric towards the body and overcast these wires securely at the back. Bend and shape the wings to suit the insect.

Clever concepts with wire-edged taffeta ribbon

Ribbon techniques

This butterfly relies on sensitive manipulation of the wired edge of the taffeta ribbon.

Materials required
Wire-edged taffeta ribbon
Metallic thread
Embroidery thread: stranded cotton/floss
No 8/9 between needle
Sharp scissors
Pins

1   Cut a length of ribbon, slightly longer than the illustrated wing (use the template below). Pull up the wire very tightly on one side and more gently on the other side. Gauge the size from the sketch. Coil the wire on itself so that the gathers can't pull out and roll the raw edges under on either side. Slip hem these edges in place.

2   Decorate the ribbon wing with stab stitch veins in antique silver/black metallic thread. Make up four wings and then choose a position on the background fabric for the butterfly. Embroider the body and feelers as follows:

   Head: Colonial knots, silver/black metallic thread.
   Thorax (body): bullions, charcoal floss (2 strands)
   Abdomen: Double-sided cast-on buttonhole, charcoal floss (2 strands).
   Feelers: Extended French knots, silver/black metallic thread (single strand).

3   Now assemble the wings to fit the body shape. Slip hem into position.

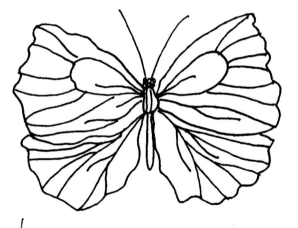

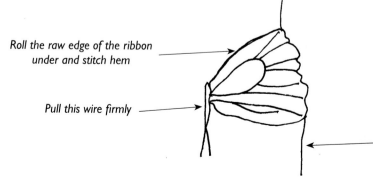

Roll the raw edge of the ribbon under and stitch hem

Pull this wire firmly

Pull this wire gently to create soft flutes

A dash of beading

The perfect finishing touch

Beads offer embroidery that extra shimmer and gleam that is so often needed for a highlight or a touch of glamour. There are marvellous books available on traditional beading and bead techniques from simple to advanced. In *Just stitch* we would like to share the delicate inclusion of beads with the embroidered stitch, suggesting areas which are ideal for beads.

Fauna

In the animal kingdom all creatures have eyes that glisten and are perfect for bead interpretation; in the insect world of creepy crawlies (dragonflies, butterflies, beetles, bees and ladybirds), the wings, abdomen and thorax are enhanced by delicate bead detail. The effect of strung beads, like a necklace, can be seen in the dragonflies on tulle technique on page 49. Birds need a touch of glass to enhance the intrinsic beauty of the feathers, eyes and claws. The scales of fish, crabs and marine crustaceans are easily interpreted with sequins, bugle and tiny seed beads.

Flora

Beads offer the needle crafter the "wow" factor for that special finish of elements from the plant kingdom. The centres of flowers (stamens, pistil and stigmas) translate easily with beads (see projects with the passion flower on page 131). Drizzle stitch with a tiny seed bead at the tip makes a magnificent stamen.

Fruit and vegetables all have exciting pips, seeds and seed pods, for example the pomegranate, cherry, strawberry, fig, berries and strelitzia pod.

Grapes: some of the beads are wrapped while others are exposed for a "juicy" contrast.

Top: Dragonfly from the Glorious Insects design.
Above: Ribbon and bead detail from a fruit botanical.

Wrapped beads

Beading

Beads are available in a wide range of sizes and shapes. Wooden or plastic beads with a large hole are ideal for wrapping. Stranded cotton thread or silk ribbon is used to wrap beads. Once the covered oval or round beads are clustered together and attached to the background, they can be use as pods, peas, grapes, cherries, bird's eggs, buds, berries or acorns. In stumpwork many fruits can be interpreted by wrapping beads of the appropriate shape in a colour which suggests that fruit. Always leave a tail when beginning and ending for securing to the background.

Materials required
Beads
Embroidery thread or ribbon
Long, fine needle
Sharp scissors

1   Use a single strand of floss to wrap the bead, leaving a long tail which can be used to secure the bead and form the stalk if required. Work from top to bottom as shown, making enough wraps to cover the bead completely. The final wrap can include a tiny bead at the tip.

2   To create a stalk, attach the bead, leaving a small length of thread exposed. This length of thread can be wrapped or buttonholed to create a bulkier effect.

Hairbells from Country Feeling. Note the detached picot at the end of the wrapped bead – a real challenge!

Bird's nest detail from Country Feeling. Clustered, wrapped beads nestle into raffia thread.

Dangling beads

Individual covered beads can be attached with a small buttonhole stalk. Begin in the background fabric leaving 1,5 cm of thread which passes through the bead and is secured at the base of the bead with a small seed bead for extra dimension. Pass the needle back up through the bead and create the buttonhole stitch over the 1,5 cm stretch of thread.

Colonial knots with beads

Is it a bead or is it a stitch? Dropping a few beads into an area of colonial knots adds that extra zing by giving a matt surface a little shimmer. Note the subtle use of beads inset between cast-on buttonhole and bullions.

Bouclé with beads

Petite beads snuggle into bouclé which is ideal for African daisy centres and the agapanthus flower.

Drizzle stitch with beads

This is particularly effective for stamens and pistels as can be seen in the barbola rendition of a Clivia miniata flower below. Drozzle stitch with beads was also used in the main bloom of the agapanthus flower (see page 87).

Networking

Net or tulle is such an exciting fabric by virtue of its transparency and the regular grid created by the mesh. In the history of costume net occurs through the centuries on embroidered garments with lace inserts. Here we offer a couple of really different interpretations showing the potential of net: a really innovative colour combination, organza wings and a dash of beadwork create a bridal veil with a difference. Other applications include sheer curtains, a tea shower and a baby's bassinette net, a mosquito net and a baby's crib net.

Colour combinations can be adapted to suit the project for example white on white for a baby's crib or to embellish a small curtain which needs to block out an unsavoury view.

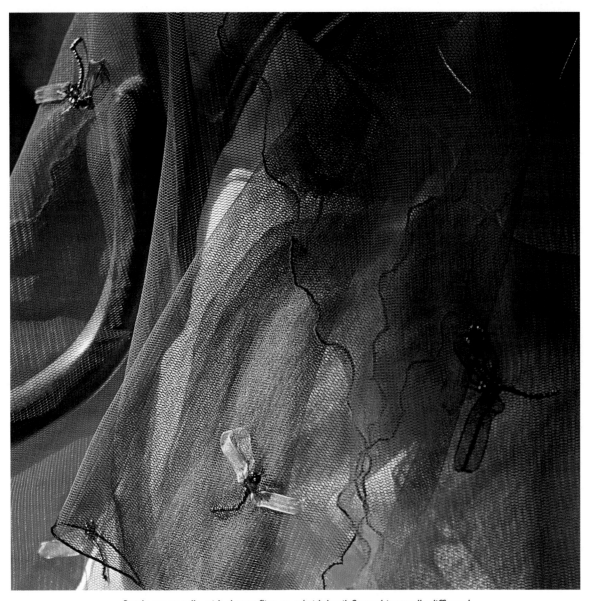

Bottle green tulle with dragonflies as a bridal veil. Something really different!

Beaded dragonflies on tulle

Make a veil with a difference

A touch of glass shimmer with beads, sheer illusion with organza ribbon and a little glitter with metallic threads, all add to the moments of magic. We used stab stitch and fly stitch for this reversible dragonfly.

Tulle, organza, batiste or other sheer background fabric
Chenille no 22, straw or bead needle no 8/9
Organza ribbon 6 mm wide in hunter green, indigo, claret, antique bronze and eau de nil
Metallic thread in antique gold
Cherry-red pebble beads, small red round beads, antique bronze beads, mixed green/indigo beads
Matches/fire lighter

1 **Start with the wings:** Use a chenille needle and thread up a short length of organza ribbon. Beginning at the thorax of the dragonfly, secure the ribbon with a couple of holding stitches in red floss. Make a 3 cm stab stitch with the organza ribbon and gently pull the ribbon through the tulle without damaging the weave. Pull through to the other side forming the right-hand side of the wings on both sides of the tulle. Do not cut the ribbon yet.

2 **Add the thorax:** Pass the ribbon through a cherry size bead creating the thorax, making a few invisible stitches securing the bead with the red floss. Make another 3 cm stab stitch with the ribbon on the opposite side and return to the original starting point. Cut (sear the ribbon ends with the blue part of the flame) and secure the raw ends of the organza ribbon on the underside of the tulle. Cover the join on this side with six to seven small red beads in a cluster.

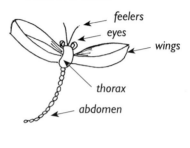

feelers — eyes — wings — thorax — abdomen

3 **The abdomen** is created by threading around 20 green/indigo beads, like a necklace, from the cherry bead thorax, a small distance away allowing a little movement. Start with a knot and backstitch inside the cherry bead. Secure the end into the tulle and return to the thorax, threading back up the string of beads excluding the first bead. End off as neatly as possible at the thorax bead.

4 **For the eyes and feelers,** attach the bronze beads with the antique black/gold metallic thread and make a small fly stitch between the beads for the feelers.

5 **Embellish the wings** with a few stab stitches in antique black/gold thread.

Mesh food covers

Make an African daisy

Even mesh food covers can be glamorous if embroidered with textured threads for an alfresco dinner!

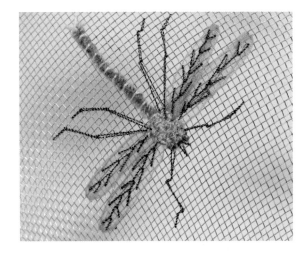

Materials required
Mesh food cover
Chenille no 22, straw or bead needle no 8/9
6 mm organza ribbon, apricot
Flat rayon ribbon, lime green
Matching machine thread
Chenille, plum red, bouclé, yellow
Yarn, plum red, yellow
Fabric glue

1   Thread the chenille needle with the lime green flat rayon ribbon, begin with a knot at the base of the sieve secured with thread and a dash of fabric glue. Count approximately 20 mesh holes and form the stem with stab stitch by piercing the chenille needle through the mesh at this point and return to the front through the very next hole. Form a pair of leaves each side of the stalk using a lazy daisy stitch. Do not cut the rayon ribbon, but repeat the technique and continue up the stalk, keeping the back as perfect as the front. End with a tight knot worked through the mesh and secure with thread and a dash of glue. The stem is approximately 50 mesh holes from the base to the edge of the petals.

2   Thread up with the organza ribbon and work the petals from the centre of the bloom from front to back in groups of 3 (3, 6, 9 o'clock) creating perfect petals on both sides of the sieve. Continue repeating the petals until 7 have been worked.

3   The centre of the bloom is couched chenille in shades of plum red yarn and finished with colonial knots. The stamens are couched yellow bouclé using matching yarn. All beginnings and endings must be immaculate on both sides.

Machine stitching

For needle crafters who enjoy machine embroidery, textured threads offer a host of possibilities.

Suggested applications

- Chenille and cords can be worked with invisible thread and zigzag stitch.
- Magnificent wall hangings can be enhanced by including machine stitched chenille, bouclé and rayon, and this becomes needlework art.
- Random top stitching of different threads onto special background fabric creates a new effect or can enhance a motif.
- Top stitching of cords and textured threads over tapestry fabric is yet another idea.
- With machine stitching a number of textured threads can be adhered to the background and left dangling which creates an instant fringe, for example knitted rayon, organza ribbon, chenille thread and wool.
- Make tassels and plaits with textured threads for key rings, earrings, shawls and tie-backs.
- Plait a number of different textured threads together, knot the ends and machine stitch them to any quilt or scatter cushion for a border finish.
- Machine stitching of textured threads on a dissoluble fabric, creates independent shapes such as seaweed, vascular systems of autumn leaves, nets and meshes.

Blombos: Some of the stalks have been machine stitched with zig-zag.

Wonderful textures created by manipulating different neutral fabrics inspired by dried husks.

A rich textured effect achieved by inserting chenille thread and cord between pin tucks.

Working with metallic threads

Fine metallic threads work best with antique goldwork methods or any number of crewel embroidery stitches.

Tips

- Couch or appliqué heavy metallic threads.
- Run metallic threads through beeswax to prevent snagging.
- Mixed black and gold or black and silver thread is an ideal medium for feelers, veins, insect legs and bodies.

- For a very fine effect separate one of the strands from this mercerised type thread and work with one strand only.

oyster

inspiration

projects

Metalasia muricata

Lesley Turpin-Delport

Blombos

Blombos and dragonflies

Application: Framed picture

Blombos or white bristle bush (*Metalasia muricata*) is a dune shrub indigenous to the coastal and mountainous areas of the Western Cape. It belongs to the fynbos group of plants known for their small flowers and needle-like leaves. This design combines free-style stitchery, textured threads and traditional threads.

Materials required

Background fabric (cotton or linen)
Muslin/cotton voile (foundation fabric)

Needles

Straw no 7/8
Chenille no 22/24 for ribbon work
Between no 7/8

A selection of embroidery thread

Stranded cotton (floss): Variegated pink, shades of green, variegated blue
Perlé: Blue/green, olive green, oyster white, white
Metallic thread: Antique black/gold

Textured threads

Chenille: Evergreen, oyster white, mink, pink, olive green, lime green, apricot
Rayon cord: Evergreen, olive green, lime green, brown, cream
Fine yarn: Evergreen, olive green, lime green, brown, pink, cream, apricot

Silk ribbon

Shades of green, olive and hunter

Miscellaneous

Scraps of hand-dyed silk
Appliqué paper
Tiny brown beads
Water-soluble crayons

Instructions

Transfer the design on page 141 onto your fabric and prepare the fabric as described on page 17. Study the photograph of the embroidered design and refer to the stitch glossary (page 134) and techniques (page 14) for finer details.

Hint: Background fabric can be painted before you begin stitching.

BLOMBOS

1 **Buds:** We suggest several options to allow for visual and textured illusions and to create a depth of field:
   a. Extended French knots; white, ecru and pink perlé/yarn/floss (single strand).
   b. Bullion, lazy-daisy and bullion rosebuds; white, ecru and pink perlé/yarn/floss (single strand).
   c. Stab/fly stitch and colonial knots; white, ecru and pink perlé/yarn/floss (single strand).
   d. Bullions and Colonial knots, khaki and ochre yarn/floss (2 strands).

2 **Full blown blooms:** Couched chenille, pink, oyster white, mink and apricot couched in matching yarn.

3 **Depleted blooms:** Fly and extended fly stitch, shades of green, white and ecru perlé/yarn or floss (single strand).

4 **Stems:** We suggest several options:
   a. Beige, brown and off-white various rayon cords couched in matching yarn/floss (single strand).
   b. Coral stitch, green and brown perlé/yarn/floss (2 strands).

5 **Leaves:** We suggest several options:
   a. Stab stitch, variegated green silk ribbon.

Stitches used (see Stitch glossary page 134)

Couching, extended french knots, bullion, lazy-daisy and bullion rosebuds, stab stitch, colonial knots, fly stitch, extended fly stitch, coral stitch, 3-spoke woven picot, buttonhole, tufting, backstitch, feather stitch, bullion rosebuds, 2-spoke woven picot

Techniques used (see New dimensions page 14)

Creative threads, silk appliqué, ribbon techniques

b. Lazy daisy, variegated green perlé/floss.

c. Bullions, evergreen and hunter green yarn/floss (single strand).

d. Woven picot, variegated green perlé.

6 **Foliage:** Evergreen chenille couched with loops in matching yarn/floss (single strand).

DRAGONFLIES

I **Silk appliqué:** Follow the instructions for this technique on page 23 and iron the silk shapes onto the embroidery background. Complete the appliqué process by buttonholing the raw edge of the wings in matching/variegated floss, using a single strand. This secures the raw edge and prevents fraying.

2 **Decorate the wings** by adding veins in feather stitch or by couching long stab stitch in matching shades of silk/floss. Once the wings are complete, use textured stitches to work the body.

3 **Head/eyes:** Bullion rosebuds (4, 6 wraps), toning silk floss (single strand).

4 **Feeler:** Fly stitch, antique black/gold metallic thread (half strand).

5 **Thorax:** Colonial knots, toning colours (single strand); options: chenille thread or tufting.

6 **Legs:** Backstitch, metallic black/gold or black/silver (half strand).

7 **Abdomen:** There are several stitch options for the abdomen, depending on how textured and wide you want it:

a. Short, horizontal bullions, changing colour every 3 to 4 bullions and increasing or reducing the number of wraps to create the irregular shapes (double and single strand).

b. Pairs of vertical bullions, tapering to one and ending with a fly stitch, toning colours (double and single strand).

8 **Background:** Lightly wash the background with watercolour crayons or fabric paint for soft shadows (optional).

Quick 'n easy dragonfly

Application: Pyjamas or beach gear

Glamorise a pair of pyjamas or a beach shirt by embroidering oyster white dragonflies on the pocket, back yoke and cuffs of the pants. This quick and easy design uses oyster white yarn and two small pearl beads.

Materials required
Pyjamas or beach shirt
Needles
Straw needle no 7/8, crewel needle no 7/8 and bead needle no 9/10
Textured thread
Yarn: oyster white
Miscellaneous
Beads: small pearl white
Sharp HB pencil

Instructions

Use the template on page 142 and lightly sketch the design onto those parts of the pyjamas you wish to embellish.

1 **Wings:** Outline in chain stitch, oyster white yarn.
2 **Veins on wings:** Feather stitch, oyster white yarn.
3 **Thorax:** Colonial knots, oyster white yarn.
4 **Abdomen:** Bullions, approximately 9 wraps, oyster white yarn in pairs then taper with single bullions finishing off with a fly stitch.
5 **Eyes:** Pearl beads.
6 **Feelers:** Fly stitch, oyster white yarn.

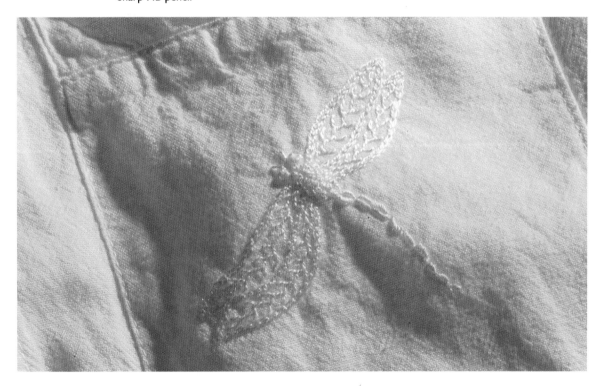

Stitches used (see Stitch glossary on page 134)
Chain stitch, feather stitch, colonial knots, bullions, fly stitch
Techniques used (see New dimensions page 14)
Beading

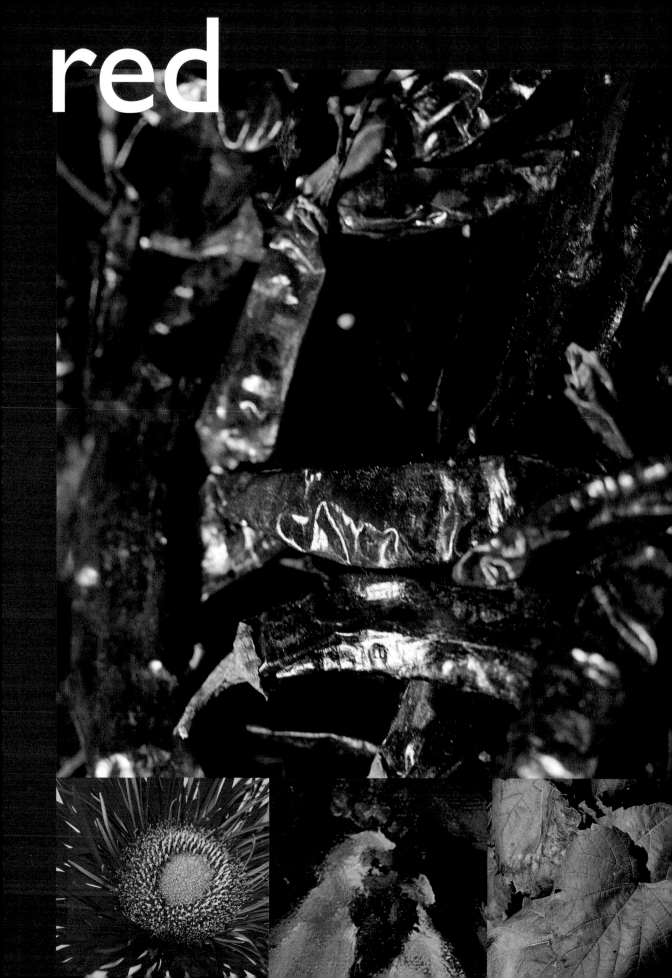

red

inspiration

projects

Three-dimensional gerbera

Application: decorative flower arrangement or a bridal boquet

This embroidery was inspired by our love of the gerbera flower, named in honour of Traugott Gerber, a German naturalist. *Gerbera jamesonii*, also known as the Transvaal or Barberton daisy, is an indigenous South African perennial, widely grown as an ornamental flowering plant for its exquisite blooms. Long-lasting gerberas are the fifth most important cut flower in the world. The leaves are woolly on their undersides and radiate out from a central growing point in a rosette fashion. The stalks are topped with single daisy-like flower heads up to 10 cm across. Gerberas come in many sizes with colours ranging from white and yellow to orange, pink and red.

Materials required
Felt (thick and thin) red and green
Red organdy fabric, dyed cotton and silk dupion

Needles
Tapestry no 22, chenille no 18-22, straw no 4/5 and embroidery no 7/8

Ribbons
Variegated red silk, 4 mm and 7 mm wide

A selection of threads
Stranded Cotton: variegated red, green
Perlé: variegated red, variegated green

Textured threads
Yarn: burgundy and yellow
Chenille: yellow
Bouclé: red/black and yellow

Miscellaneous
Embroidery hoops, 10/15 cm (4/6 in)
Anti-fray glue
Sharp scissors
Wire, gauge 28/18
Appliqué paper
Wadding

Instructions

The bloom is made up of three whorls of petals. Each whorl is cut on double fabric so choose the combinations to suit the most attractive colours. The thicker fabric should be at the base, with the most flimsy towards the top. The centre of the bloom is a circle of felt, embellished with stamens and fresh petal growth. Use the template on page 144.

1 Using the template on page 144, follow the appliqué instructions on page 23 and prepare 2 x whorl 1 on silk dupion and 1 x whorl 2 on cotton (with appliqué backing paper still intact). Cut out carefully. Remove the backing paper of one cotton and one silk dupion whorl and iron them onto the organza. Put the organdy fabric into an embroidery hoop. Buttonhole around the outer edges in variegated red stranded cotton, single strand. Keep the stitches regular in size and space. Apply anti-fray around the shapes on the organdy fabric just touching the stitches, allow to dry and cut out as close to the stitching as possible.

2 Iron the remaining silk whorl onto thick red felt, cut out and buttonhole around the edge using single strand variegated cotton.

3 Cut a 1,5 cm cross in the centre of each petal whorl and buttonhole to prevent fraying.

4 **Gerbera centre:** Use the template on page 144 and transfer the centre circle onto the thin red felt. Do not cut out. Place the felt into a small hoop. Couch the yellow chenille in a circular motion using the matching yarn until the shape is a third filled (see diagram c, page 145). Couch the red/black and yellow bouclé next to the centre filling the rest of the shape. (Optional: use the burgundy yarn and add drizzle stitch into the bouclé – cast on 5 to 7

Stitches used (see Stitch glossary page 134)
Buttonhole, looped three-dimensional petal, wire-woven picot, 2-spoke woven picot, running stitch/gather, couching, drizzle stitch, colonial knots

Techniques used (see New dimensions, page 14)
Textured threads, felt, exposed felt, dimensional picot petals, silk ribbon

loops). Use the 4 mm silk ribbon to create looped three-dimensional petals (see Ribbon stitches page 140) around the bouclé, securing the ribbon with a colonial knot at the base of each petal with 2 strands of red stranded cotton or burgundy yarn. Behind that row stitch a second row of looped three-dimensional petals in 7 mm silk ribbon and secure with colonial knots in red stranded cotton (2 strands) or burgundy yarn. Run a gathering thread 2,5 cm (½ in) away around the embroidery. Remove from hoop and push a little wadding into the cavity as you draw up the gathering threads. Cut away any excess felt.

5 **Dimensional picot petals:** Cut the wire into 9 x 15 cm lengths and make nine dimensional picot petals as described in New dimensions page 34. Use variegated red perlé. You will be left with two tails on each petal for connection around the centre stamens. If holding the wire is difficult connect the wire shape to a fabric base with tacking stitches. Weave the wire and cut away the holding stitches on completion..

6 **Calyx and stem:** Use the template on page 144 and cut out sections 3, 4 and 5 from the green felt.

7 **Assemble the gerbera:** Follow the steps on page 38 to assemble the gerbera.

Bougainvillea

Application: Framed picture, soft furnishing focus

Named after Louis Antoine de Bougainville who discovered this popular ornamental plant in Brazil in 1768, the bougainvillea bears clusters of tiny flowers surrounded by papery bracts in many vibrant colours. This spectacular three-dimensional bougainvillea branch is true-to-life in size, shape and colour. Learn to mould the bracts with wired and unwired three-dimensional techniques and enhance the centres with an array of fabulous stitches.

Materials required

Background fabric

Muslin (foundation fabric)

Off-cuts of mottled green and pink/burgundy cotton fabric for appliqué

Off-cuts of peachy pink, burgundy and red, silk dupion and red organza

Needles

Straw/milliners no 8/9, between no 9/10

crewel no 7/8

A selection of embroidery threads

Stranded cotton (floss): olive green, khaki, dark green, yellow, ochre, grey-blue, pinky-brown and several shades of peachy pink through scarlet to burgundy red

Perlé: several shades of peachy pink through scarlet to burgundy red, grey-blue, rust, pinky-brown and khaki

Ribbon

Variegated pink/burgundy/red wire-edged taffeta 25 mm wide

Miscellaneous

Appliqué paper/Vilene

Pink, burgundy or red beads and/or flower-shaped beads

Red wire gauge 28-32

Anti-fray glue

Hoop

Instructions

The bougainvillea flower is a complex structure. The pink/red coloured leaves which we will refer to as the bloom are clusters of three bracts. Their centres are actually the flowers. There are three tiny protrusions with minute floral tips per cluster of bracts. Transfer the design on page 143 to your background fabric and prepare the fabric for embroidery as described on page 17. Use the photographs as a guide and refer to the stitch glossary and techniques section for details

Stitches used (see Stitch glossary page 134)

Romanian, bullions, buttonhole, coral stitch, long and short split stitch, couching, vertical spider's web, cast-on buttonhole, double-sided cast-on buttonhole, whipped chain, drizzle stitch, stab stitch, stem stitch, lazy daisy, running

Techniques used (see New dimensions page 14)

Appliqué, wire techniques (elevated shapes)

BACKGROUND EMBROIDERY

1 **Main stem:** Coral stitch in pinky-brown perlé (single strand).

2 **Smaller stems:** Whipped chain in pinky-brown floss (single strand) branching into bullions at the base of the bloom. Bullions, about 15 wraps in yellow floss (single strand).

3 **Free standing stem (barbola bloom):** Cast-on buttonhole stalk in pinky-brown perlé. The dried calyxes at the base of the barbola bloom are drizzle stitch in ochre floss (single strand).

4 **Thorns:** Bullions, about 9 wraps in pinky-brown floss (single strand).

5 **Appliquéd leaves:** Appliqué the leaves in mottled green fabric. Position leaves, embroider the outline of each leaf shape in buttonhole with matching green floss (single strand). Central vein: whipped chain, olive green floss (2 strands). Small veins: long bullions, olive green floss (single strand). Shadows are satin stitch in dark green floss (single strand).

6 **Smaller leaves:** Romanian in olive and dark green floss (2 strands).

7 **Flat appliquéd blooms:** Appliqué blooms in the range of peachy-pink dyed cotton, silk dupion and organza. Position blooms and embroider the outline of each shape in buttonhole with matching floss (single strand). Delineate veins in whipped chain/bullions in matching floss (single strand) and petal divisions in stem stitch in matching floss (single strand).

THREE-DIMENSIONAL BLOOMS

1 **Silk, organza and cotton blooms:** Use template on page 142 and trace the shapes of blooms on appliqué paper (2 of each size). Cut red wire-veins for bracts (3 for each bloom). Lie wire in centre of petal, from tip to stalk. Follow techique for silk appliqué with fabrics selected. When you peel off the paper, place wire central veins into position before ironing the two sections together. Set aside medium-size silk bloom for barbola. Buttonhole raw edges using matching floss (single strand). Apply anti-fray glue to edges, allow to dry, cut out the shape. Whip over the wire which becomes the central vein. Stab stitch both sides of the bracts creating smaller veins

using matching floss (single strand). Bend and shape blooms into position and catch the bracts together for 1 cm from base of bloom.

2 **Barbola bloom:** Put prepared fabric with medium-sized bloom into a hoop and follow instructions on page 26. Once the shape has been filled, whip over the wire which becomes the central vein. Bend and shape bloom into position and catch the bracts together for about 1 cm from the base of the flower.

3 **Taffeta bloom:** Cut 3 trapezium shapes, 10 cm on the longer side, from taffeta ribbon. Sear diagonal sides under flame to prevent fraying. Gently pull the wire from the shorter length, leaving the wire in the longer length to help with shaping later on. Gather each piece of ribbon with small running stitches around the 3 shorter sides leaving the longest side. Connect the 3 bracts together slightly overlapping each other. Stitch up the sides of each bract for about 1 cm and fold the wired edge into shape.

CENTRAL FLOWERS AND SHAFTS

There are several options:

1 Drizzle stitch (about 25 cast-ons) using matching floss or slightly darker floss (double strand), the starting point 5 mm from the base of the central vein. It is optional to add a bead onto the top of the cast-ons before rethreading the needle and pulling through the fabric.

2 Drizzle stitch (about 25 cast-ons) using matching perlé or darker perlé. It is optional to add a glass flower bead onto the top of the cast-ons before rethreading the needle and pulling through the fabric.

3 To create the tiny flower at the top of the drizzle stitch, bring the yellow floss or perlé (depending on what you used for the drizzle stitch – floss or perlé) up the central shaft of the drizzle stitch. Hook the first lazy daisy into the top cast-on and continue around the top of the drizzle stitch making 5 separate tiny petals (don't pull too hard or the lazy daisy collapses). Go back down the centre shaft of the drizzle stitch and end off.

4 Central flowers inside the barbola bloom are single-strand cast-on buttonhole loops in yellow floss worked onto the tip of the drizzle stitch.

green

inspiration

projects

Nesting weaver

Application: framed picture

Rendering a red-headed weaver (*Anaplectes melanotis*) in embroidery is great fun as both the bird and its nest offer so much scope for creativity. This interpretation is a combination of fine embroidery techniques and textured three-dimensional effects. The foliage is hand appliqué, embellished with chenille and cords. The nest is intertwined wool, raffia, chenille and bouclé, encasing the trapunto bird of fine needle painting and textured threads, suggesting feathers.

Materials required
Background fabric, 35x35 cm
Muslin (foundation fabric)
Needles
Chenille no 18-22, straw no 7/8, beading no 9/10
A selection of embroidery threads
Stranded cotton (floss): olive green, pinky brown, oyster beige, scarlet/orange, yellow and charcoal grey
Textured threads
Bouclé: cream/ecru, mottled brown, pale green, mottled green
Yarn: toffee brown, evergreen, brown, ochre, lime green, cream/ecru and olive green
Chenille: ochre, toffee brown and evergreen
Crazy wools: shaggy green, shaggy brown
Rayon cord (round): gold and brown
Knitted rayon (flat): olive green, lime green and ochre
Ribbon
Organza: copper, 6 mm wide
Miscellaneous
Small piece of mottled green fabric for appliqué
Appliqué paper or Vilene
1 metallic bead for the eye

Instructions

Transfer the design on page 145 onto your fabric and prepare the fabric as described on page 17. Study the photograph of the embroidered design and refer to the stitch glossary and techniques for finer details.

Options: This design can be painted (see page 12) or photo transferred (see page 16) before stitching.

1   **Body outline:** Backstitch in the colour matching the appropriate area (single strand). Trapunto quilt the body and wing (see page 35).
2   **Breast:** Split stitch in oyster beige floss (single strand).
3   **Crown:** Split stitch in scarlet/orange floss (single strand). Add stab stitch details in yellow floss (single strand).
4   **Cheek:** Couch in ochre chenille with the matching yarn.
5   **Beak:** Split stitch in bright yellow floss (single strand).
6   **Eye:** Cast-on-buttonhole lids in brown yarn finishing with a metallic petite bead in the centre.
7   **Upper body back:** Couch mottled green bouclé with matching yarn.
8   **Lower body back:** Couch light green bouclé with matching yarn and add detail with bullions in charcoal grey floss (single strand).
9   **Wings:** Stab stitch organza ribbon, embellish with stan stitch (yellow floss, singel strand) and highlight with stab stitch ostrich feather detail.
10 **Tail feathers:** Stab stitch in organza ribbon culminating in cast-on-buttonhole loops in cream/ecru yarn and detail stab stitch in yellow floss (single strand).
11 **Leg:** Vertical spider's web in pinky brown floss (2 strands).

Stitches used (see Stitch glossary page 134)
Stab stitch, couching, bullions, buttonhole, vertical spider's web, cast-on buttonhole, split stitch, backstitch
Techniques (see New dimensions page 14)
Textured threads, appliqué, trapunto

12 **Claw:** Bullion, about 9 wraps in pinky brown floss (single strand).

13 **Leaves:** Appliqué the leaves in mottled green fabric (see page 23). Once the leaves have been ironed and tacked into position, embroider the outline of each leaf shape in buttonhole with green floss (single strand). The central vein of the larger leaves can be couched with green rayon cord with invisible stitches. The small veins are long bullions in olive green floss (single strand). Add texture by couching evergreen chenille over the buttonhole using matching yarn. Softly butt the shaggy chenille up against the outline by couching.

14 **Nest:** Select one of the brown chenille threads and couch a basic nest shape around the bird by referring to the main picture. At the top of the leaf mass, secure and pull through a selection of appropriate nest threads (chenille, bouclé, raffia and rayon cord (flat and round)) in the various shades of brown, ochre and beige. Twist, plait and manipulate the textured threads into an interesting nest shape and secure couching in place in matching thread (see Working with textured threads, page 18).

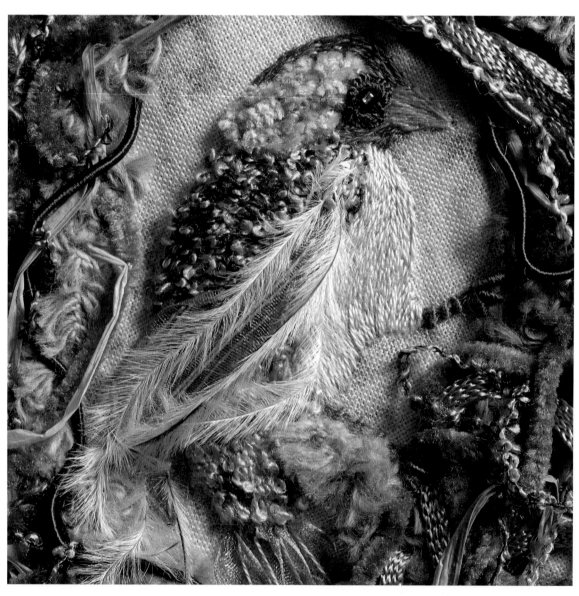

Quick 'n easy mantis magic

Application: cushion, framed picture, mesh food-cover, laundry bag, napkins

Play with the dynamic contrast of sheer organza and the tactile quality of chenille, bouclé, rayon and yarn. The techniques are simple: couching and a few traditional crewel stitches combined with a freedom of spirit and a fun-filled approach to traditional stitchery.

Materials required
Damask background fabric (cotton/linen or silk) 50x50 cm
Cotton voile (foundation fabric)
Needles
Straw no 7/8, chenille 18, beading 9/10
A selection of embroidery threads
Stranded cotton (floss): shades of green (lime to hunter green)
Textured threads
Chenille: evergreen
Bouclé: evergreen
Fine yarn: evergreen
Ribbon
Organza: evergreen, 6 mm wide
Miscellaneous
Tiny yellow beads

Instructions

Use the template on page 147 and transfer the design to the embroidery fabric. Study the photograph and use the stitch glossary for reference and enjoy a creative, mixed media experience.

1 **Head:** Padded satin stitch, lime to hunter green floss (single strand).
2 **Eyes:** Tiny yellow beads.
3 **Feelers:** Couched stab stitch, lime green floss (single strand).
4 **Thorax:** Evergreen bouclé and chenille couched with matching yarn.
5 **Abdomen:** Couched evergreen bouclé and chenille couched with bullion details, lime to hunter green floss (single and 2 strands).
6 **Wing:** Stab stitch, evergreen organza ribbon.
7 **Upper leg segments:** Cast-on buttonhole, lime to hunter green floss (2 strands).
8 **Middle leg segments:** Bullions, lime to hunter green floss (2 strands).
9 **Lower leg segments:** Fly stitch, lime to hunter green floss (single and 2 strands).

Stitches used (see Stitch glossary page 134)
Padded satin stitch, couching, bullions, stab stitch, cast-on buttonhole, fly stitch
Techniques (see New dimensions page 14)
Textured threads, ribbon techniques, beading

yellow

inspiration

projects

NW2005

Prickly poppy

Application: framed picture.

This design was inspired by an antique topographical drawing. The plant is *Argemone mexicana*, a species of poppy from mexico. The two species of beetle are the long-horned beetle, *Callipogon cinnamoneus*, and its fleshy larva in the centre of the plant, and the large brown beetle, *Taeniotes farinosus*, including a flying specimen and a small larva. Enjoy a free-style embroidery project, exploring the potential of creative threads in different textures.

Materials required
Background fabric (cotton or linen), 50x60 cm
Muslin (foundation fabric)
Needles
No 7/8 straw, no 22 chenille, fine bead needle
A selection of embroidery threads
Stranded cotton (floss): matching shades of green, khaki, mustard/yellow, brown, oyster white, ginger, black
Metallic thread: black/gold
Textured threads
Chenille: cream, brown
Bouclé: evergreen, hunter green, mottled green, cream, brown, ginger
Rayon cord (round): brown, oyster white, mustard, ginger
Kinitted rayon (flat): evergreen
Fine yarn: cream, evergreen, olive, hunter green, mustard, dark brown, black
Ribbon
Organza: brown, mustard, cinnamon, oyster-pink
Miscellaneous
Small opaque brown beads
Soutache (brown and mustard)

Instructions

Transfer the design on page 148 onto your background fabric and prepare the fabric as detailed on page 17. Study the photograph and the stitch glossary. Where possible, work the traditional embroidery first, (the stems, legs, feelers), then move on to the textured areas, finishing with the ribbon work.

PLANT

1 **Main stems:** Chain stitch, shades of green yarn (single strand).
2 **Leaves:** Large veins couched rayon cord, evergreen; leaf filler couched bouclé, shades of green and

Stitches used (see Stitch glossary page 134)
Chain stitch, couching, bullions, stab stitch, cast-on buttonhole, overcast stem, stem stitch, fly stitch, colonial knot, double-sided cast on buttonhole
Techniques (see New dimensions page 14)
Textured threads, ribbon work

brown; fine veins and shadows chain stitch, green yarn (single strand); leaf tips bullions, shades of green yarn/floss (single strand).

3   **Flower:** Stab stitch, yellow and khaki organza ribbon with stab stitch.

4   **Petals:** Details in stab stitch, yellow and khaki floss (single strand).

5   **Pistil:** Cast-on buttonhole, yellow floss shaft (2 strands) and bullion bud, brown floss (single strand).

LONG-HORNED BEETLE

1   **Back:** Couched rayon cord, brown and ginger held down with matching floss/yarn (single strand).

2   **Outline:** Overcast stem, dark brown yarn.

3   **Head:** Couched brown chenille with colonial knot and bullion filler, brown and ginger floss (single strand).

4   **Detail:** Tiny, brown beads for eyes.

5   **Pinchers:** Cast-on buttonhole, brown floss (2 strands).

6   **Feelers:** Chain stitch, ginger floss (single strand) with colonial knots or tiny brown beads towards the broad end.

7   **Legs:** Bullions, brown floss (2 strands).

8   **Abdomen:** Cream chenille with bullion and colonial knot details in beige and black floss (single strand).

FLYING BEETLE

1   **Head:** Bullions and colonial knots, dark brown and mustard floss (single strand).

2   **Abdomen:** Couched brown chenille with bullion, mustard floss (single strand).

3   **Legs and feelers:** Overcast stem, dark brown floss (single strand).

4   **Wings:** Stab stitch, brown and oyster-pink organza ribbon decorated with fly stitch and and colonial knots in brown metallic thread and pinky beige floss (single strand).

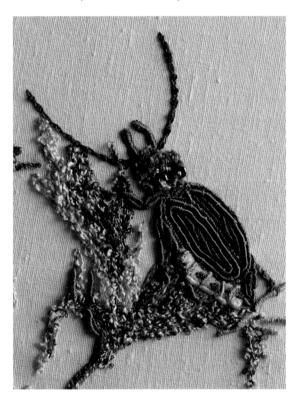

FLESHY LARVA

Couched cream chenille thread embellished with khaki-coloured bullion details, tiny brown beads and colonial knots

LARGE BROWN BEETLE

1 **Back:** Couched rayon cord (round), donkey brown and mustard, held down with matching floss/yarn (single strand).
2 **Pinchers:** Bullions, dark brown floss (single strand).
3 **Eyes:** Bullions, shades of brown floss (single strand) and tiny brown beads.
4 **Feelers:** Chain stitch, brown floss (single strand) with colonial knots, mustard floss (single strand).
5 **Legs:** Bullions, colonial knots and stab stitch, dark brown and mustard floss (single strand).

SMALL LARVA

1 **Body:** Couched beige rayon cord (round), held in place with beige yarn bullions.
2 **Head and tail:** Stab stitch, donkey brown yarn (single strand)

Quick 'n easy insects

Application: Children's clothes, hand towels, cocktail napkins and jeans

Bugs and other small creatures are quick and easy embroidery projects and can be used to personalise and embellish any nuber of fuunctional items. We give you instructions for several insects and the rolled-picot snail. Use the photograph as a guide and your imagination to embroider the rest of the bugs.

Materials required
Background fabric or item to be decorated
Needles
Straw no 7/8/9
Chenille no 22
Crewel no 8
A selection of embroidery threads
Stranded cotton (floss): pinky brown, yellow, pink
Perlé: variegated brown
Metallic thread: antique black/gold
Floss: pinky brown
Textured threads
Chenille: yellow and brown
Ribbon
Organza: yellow, 6 mm wide

Instructions

Use the template on page 152 and lightly sketch the design onto the background fabric or those parts of the clothing or other items you wish to embellish.

BULLION BUTTERFLIES

1 **Wings:** Upper, bullion loops about 30 wraps, pink, blue and yellow floss (2 strands); lower, bullion loops about 25 wraps, matching or contrast floss (2 strands).
2 **Abdomen:** Bullion bar about 9 wraps, toning or contrasting floss (2 strands).
3 **Feelers:** Extended French knots, antique black/gold metallic thread (half strand).

PICOT SNAIL

1 **Body:** Colonial knots, pinky brown floss (2 strands).
2 **Shell:** Rolled 2-spoke picot, vriegated brown perlé. Start the picot in the centre of the shell and work to 6 cm (2½ in) in length. On completion of the picot, roll and shape to form the shell, slip stitching in position as you roll.
3 **Feelers:** Extended French knots, antique black/gold metallic thread (half strand).

BUMBLE BEE

1 **Wings:** Stab stitch, organdy ribbon with metallic black/gold, stab stitch details (single strand).
2 **Body:** Turkey work/tufting, ochre and brown floss (2 strands).
3 **Legs:** Back stitch, black/gold metallic thread (half strand).
4 **Head and feelers:** colonial knots and extended French knots, antique black/gold metallic thread.

Stitches used (see Stitch glossary page 134)
Colonial knots, Turkey work (tufting), bullion, stab stitch, slip stitch, 2-spoke picot, extended French knots, back stitch
Techniques used (see New dimensions page 14)
Metallic thread, ribbon techniques

blue

inspiration

projects

Brenton Blue butterflies

Applications: framed picture, guest towels, bath towels, lid of a trinket jewellery box

This series of butterflies is based on the Brenton Blue (*Orachrysops niobe*) a threatened and nearly extinct species whose natural habitat is the coastal area of Brenton-on-Sea near the Southern Cape coastal town Knysna. Enjoy a new approach to ribbon embroidery in the creation of the design with a sensitive use of metallic thread.

Materials required
Silk, cotton or damask background fabric
Muslin (foundation fabric)
Dupion silk, lilac/blue for wings

A selection of embroidery threads
Stranded cotton (floss) or hand-dyed silk: lilac/blue (jacaranda), shades of brown, beige, grey, white, charcoal
Metallic thread: antique black/silver, white

Ribbon
Hand-dyed silk ribbon in shades of brown and lilac/blue 3,5 mm wide

Needles
Straw/milliners no 7/8 for bullions and buttonhole
Crewel no 7/8 for general embroidery
Chenille no 22-24 for ribbon work

Miscellaneous
Embroidery hoop
Appliqué paper
Thin silver wire
Artificial stamens
Small burgundy beads

Instructions

For this pure silk interpretation, transfer the designs on page 149 to the background fabric and prepare the fabric as detailed on page 17. Study the photographs, the labelled template on page 149 and the stitch glossary and create the wonderful indigenous butterflies illustrated.

SILK RIBBON BUTTERFLY (FLAT RENDITION))

1 **Wings:** Stab stitch the basic shape in lilac/blue silk ribbon. Control the ribbon and decorate the wings following the coloured picture.
2 **Upper edge:** Overcast stem stitch, lilac silk thread/floss (single strand).
3 **Outer edge:** Buttonhole, grey silk thread/floss (single strand).
4 **Wing division:** Overcast stem, grey silk thread/floss (single strand).
5 **Veins:** Stab stitch and couching, lilac and plum silk thread/floss (single strand).
6 **Shading:** Long and sort satin stitch, lilac/blue silk thread/floss (single strand).
7 **Feelers:** Stem stitch and bullions, light grey and lilac silk thread/floss (single strand).
8 **Head:** Petite burgundy beads and colonial knots, charcoal grey silk thread/floss (single strand).
9 **Thorax:** Bullions, light grey and lilac silk thread/floss (single strand).
10 **Abdomen:** Double-sided cast-on buttonhole, charcoal silk thread/floss (2 strands).

ELEVATED BUTTERFLY (WIRED WINGS)

1 Stretch a small piece of pure silk or fine cotton into the embroidery ring and follow the steps on page 28, using the thin silver wire, to the point where the

Stitches used (see Stitch glossary page 134)
Stab stitch, overcast stem, bullions, colonial knots, stem stitch, tufting (turkey work), double-sided buttonhole, long and short satin stitch, satin stitch, couching, buttonhole, lazy daisy, back stitch

Techniques used (see New dimensions page 14)
Ribbon work, elevated shapes (wire work)

wire is couched in position. Buttonhole/wrap a single strand of lilac thread over the wire and through the fabric on the upper and lower edges of the wing. Buttonhole the outer edge of the wired wing with white metallic thread. The wire will now be stable.

2   Satin stitch in light grey floss (single strand) just inside the buttonholed edge. Add the veins by making a long stab stitch in metallic silver/black thread from the front around to the back and then control the shape of the vein with couching. Leave long threads at the beginning and end, at the narrow edge of the wing. These threads can be worked into the background on completion. Create all four wings on the blue silk using the colour picture as your guide. Cut out as described on page 28.

3   Lightly sketch the body on the background fabric and embroider:

   a. Head: Colonial knots, charcoal floss (2 strands).

   b. Thorax: Long bullions, grey/brown floss (2 strands).

   c. Abdomen: Short bullions, grey/brown floss (single strand).

   d. Feelers: Stamens from artificial flowers or wrapped wire or stem stitch and colonial knots in antique silver/black metallic thread.

4   Position the wings at the thorax by pushing the wire through the fabric, bending the wire backwards and securing it with the long threads left from the embroidery.

SIDE VIEW (BROWN SILK RIBBON UNDERSIDE)

1   **Wings:** Stab stitch in hand-dyed, brown silk ribbon. Control the ribbon with decorative embroidery in

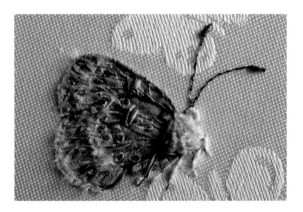

beige floss (single strand); the upper edge in overcast stem and the outer edge in spaced buttonhole. The veins are couched beige silk thread with details of spots in stab stitch, colonial knots and bullions in dark brown floss (single strand). Add a few highlights around the colonial knots with lazy daisy in white metallic thread.

2   **Feelers:** Stem stitch and bullion knots, silver/black metallic thread.

3   **Head:** Colonial knot, charcoal floss (single strand), and bullion, white floss (single strand).

4   **Thorax:** Turkey work (tufting), beige floss (2 strands).

5   **Abdomen:** Double-sided cast-on buttonhole, light brown floss (2 strands).

6   **Legs:** Bullions, white floss (single strand) with brown metallic highlights in stab stitch.

7   Complete the butterfly by defining the two wings with brown metallic backstitch. Thread an ostrich feather (from a feather duster) through the buttonhole on the outer edge and a third in from the edge, passing the feather under the couched veins.

Agapanthus

Application: scatter cushion, quilt and framed picture.

This interpretation of the *Agapanthus africanus* is magnificent for a tactile cushion. Further interpretations are suggested in New dimensions (see pages 21, 24, 26). The head of the agapanthus has several components: the bud, half open bud, the full bloom and the spent flowers. The basic trumpet is made up of six petals, five to six stamens, a pistil and a slim stem which supports the trumpet. The calyx is sometimes visible.

Materials required
Background fabric (linen, silk and cotton) 45x45 cm
Muslin (foundation fabric)
Needles
Straw no 7/8, chenille no 18-22, embroidery no 7/8
A selection of embroidery threads
Stranded cotton (floss): a range of greens, white, charcoal, oyster white
Perlé: variegated blue/purple perlé
Textured threads
Yarn: light blue, dark blue, brown, olive, lime, evergreen
Bouclé: lime, olive, evergreen, brown, hunter green, light and dark blue
Knitted rayon cord (flat): lime, evergreen olive green, beige, ginger
Chenille: olive, lime, evergreen, blue, oyster
Miscellaneous
Metallic grey beads

Instructions

Transfer the design on page 150 onto the background fabric and prepare the fabric for embroidery as described on page 17.

1   **Roots:** Rayon cord, beige and ginger, couched in place with invisible stitches in matching shades. Add details of couched brown bouclé and underline with off white yarn in stem stitch.

2   **Leaves:** We suggest several options to allow for visual and textured illusions and create a depth of field. Study the picture and the shading of the leaves and couch light, medium and dark combinations of the chenille, bouclé and rayon, contour for a softer effect with yarn in stem stitch and chain in shades of green yarn:
    a. Lime and olive kintted rayon cord (flat) couched with invisible stitches in matching yarn floss.
    b. Bouclé and yarn.
    c. Couched, hunter green bouclé and olive green yarn in continuous chain.
    d. Chenille, bouclé, yarn and rayon.

3   **Stem:** Couch down the centre of the olive green rayon cord with matching yarn in stem stitch.

Stitches used (see Stitch glossary page 134)
Couching, stem stitch, chain stitch, overcast stem, bullions, 2-/3-/5 spoke woven picot, extended French knots, drizzle stitch, split stitch
Techniques used (see New dimensions page 14)
Textured threads, beads

THE FLOWER HEAD

1 **Slim stem:** Stem stitch, overcast stem in variegated green floss (1 and 2 strands), olive and evergreen yarn.

2 **Calyx:** Bullions (6, 8, 8 wraps) in olive green floss (single strand).

3 **Buds:** Couched chenille in pale blue and oyster, picot (2-spoke, 3-spoke and 5-spoke) in variegated perlé.

4 **Half-open flower:** Combination of picot in variegated blue perlé.

5 **Profile flowers:** Split stitch in light, medium and dark blue floss (single and 2 strands).

6 **Profile flower stamens:** Extended French knots (single strand) in light blue, capped with a small bullion in charcoal floss (single strand).

7 **Full bloom:** Couch light and dark blue chenille with matching floss (single strand). Make long bullions (single strand) up the centre of each petal, suggesting the stripe that is seen in certain variations of Agapanthus.

8 **Full bloom pistil:** Drizzle stitch, white floss (2 strands) with a small metallic bead at the tip (double-sided drizzle).

9 **Full bloom stamens:** Drizzle stitch, pale blue floss (single strand) with a small metallic bead at the tip.

10 **Spent flowers:** Light and dark blue bouclé couched in matching floss (single strand). Begin with the dark blue bouclé outline and fill the centre with light blue bouclé. Make a long, purple/blue bullion in single strand floss, along the centre of each petal. The stamens of this flower are soft, stab stitch in white floss (single strand). Attach a small metallic grey bead to the end of each stab stitch.

This detail is from a different interpretation of the agapanthus flower, with ribbon and barbola. These techniques can be used for the design on the left if the embroidery is not on a cushion.

lilac

& lavender

inspiration

projects

Bloukeurboom

Application: Framed picture, cushions

The bloukeurboom or blossom tree, *Psoralea pinnata*, is a flowering tree-shrub found mainly in the Southern Cape. The dense sprays of fragrant mauve and lilac flowers with their blue-purple tips and the fine grey-green foliage lend themselves to exquisite interpretation in organza ribbon and textured threads.

Materials required
Background fabric (cotton or linen) 50x60 cm
Muslin (foundation fabric)
Needles
Straw no 7/8
Chenille no 22/24 for ribbon work
A selection of embroidery threads
Stranded cotton (floss): lilac, lime green, olive green, peach, plum
Perlé: variegated lilac/blue, plum/pink and lime/olive green
Textured threads
Round rayon cord: evergreen, hunter green
Knitted rayon cord (flat): lime, hunter green
Yarn: evergreen, lime, hunter green, lavender, plum/pink, peach
Ribbon
Silk in pale lilac, pale pink, blue/green, 3,5 mm wide
Organza in light and dark lilac/blue, plum/pink, peach, 3,5 mm wide
Organza in lavender, plum/pink, evergreen, hunter green, 3,5 mm wide

Instructions

Transfer the design on page 160 to your background fabric and prepare the fabric for embroidery as described on page 17. Use the photograph as a guide and refer to the stitch glossary and techniques section for details.

1 **Main stems:** Rayon cord, shades of evergreen and hunter green, couched in place with matching yarn/floss (single strand).
2 **Fine stems:** Stem stitch with a selection of yarn, perlé and stranded cotton (single and 2 strands) in evergreen, olive green and hunter green.
3 **Foliage:** Bullions, fly stitch and stem stitch with a selection of yarn, perlé or stranded cotton (double and single strand) in evergreen, olive green and hunter green

Stitches used (See stitch glossary page 134)
Stem stitch, stab stitch, fly stitch, detached chain (lazy daisy), bullion, cast-on buttonhole, couching
Techniques used (see New dimensions page 14)
Textured thread, ribbon embroidery

4 Buds

a. Tiny tight buds: Bullion centre, lilac or green floss (2 strands) with a lazy daisy around the bullion, lilac or green floss (2 strands).

b. Medium buds: Lazy daisy petals, in lilac and pink silk ribbon with fly stitch (olive rayon/silk ribbon) or bullion calyxes, shades of green yarn/floss (2 strands).

c. Plump bud: Petals of lazy daisy and stab stitch, lilac organza and silk ribbon with calyxes of bullion in green silk ribbon, perlé or yarn

5 Blooms: The plant belongs to the pea family and the flower is similar to a pea or a wisteria flower, resembling a little bonnet or *kappie*.

a. The full, back petals are stab stitch or lazy daisy in light and dark lilac/blue organza ribbon with details in lazy daisy or bullions, in light and dark lilac/blue perlé or yarn/floss (2 strands)

b. Front petals: Cast-on buttonhole or bullions, in light and dark lilac/blue perlé or yarn/floss (2 strands).

c. Full blown blooms: The flowered blooms change colour from lilac/blue to peach and plum/pink. Use the description under blooms but substitute the lilac/blue and use plum/pinks and peach in organza ribbon, perlé and yarn/floss (2 strands) combinations.

Quick 'n easy dragonfly on a lampshade

Application: Lampshade, pincushion

Textured threads, taffeta or organza appliqué and a few beads create a delightful dragonfly on luxurious dupion silk which is a charming picture during the day and illuminates at night. No foundation fabric is used if the embroidery is meant for a lampshade.

Materials required
Background fabric (dupion silk), enough to cover a lampshade
Needles
Straw no 7/8 (for bullions)
Between no 9/10 (for beads and fine stitching)
Chenille no 22 (for textured threads and ribbons)
A selection of embroidery threads
Stranded cotton/yarn: Lilac/lavender, purple
Metallic thread: antiqué black/gold
Textured thread
Chenille: lilac/lavender
Ribbon
Taffeta/organza 6 mm wide
Miscellaneous
Appliqué paper or iron-on Vilene
Bronze and purple beads
Lampshade frame
Decorative braid or round rayon cord
Fabric glue

MAKING THE LAMPSHADE

Position dragonfly in centre of frame and pin sides, creating a tight surface tension. Role seam allowance over metal framework, tucking raw edge under as you proceed and slip hem from the centre, outwards. Keep the stitches as invisible as possible creating a double casing. Glue braid or cord on the stitching line.

Instructions

Trace the design on page 149 onto the background fabric, correctly positioned for a lampshade, and make appliqué wings as described on page 23. Once the wings have been ironed onto the background fabric, the dragonfly is ready for embroidery embellishment.

1 **Wings:** Buttonhole the raw edge of the wings in matching/variegated floss, single strand. Add veins by couching in matching shades of floss/yarn.
2 **Eyes:** Pairs of bullions (6 wraps) in toning floss (2 strands), then attach purple beads in the centre of each pair of bullions with purple floss (single strand).
3 **Feelers:** Fly stitch, antiqué black/gold metallic thread (half strand).
4 **Thorax:** Colonial knots, lilac yarn/floss (2 strands). Bronze beads attached with matching floss (single strand).
5 **Abdomen:** Chenille thread couched with bullions, lilac/lavender yarn/floss (6-10 wraps, 2 strands).
6 **Legs:** Backstitch, metallic black/gold (half strand).

Stitches used (see Stitch glossary page 134)
Fly stitch, bullions, couching, back stitch, colonial knot, buttonhole, slim hemming
Techniques used (see New dimensions page 14)
Appliqué, textured threads, beads

salmon

inspiration

projects

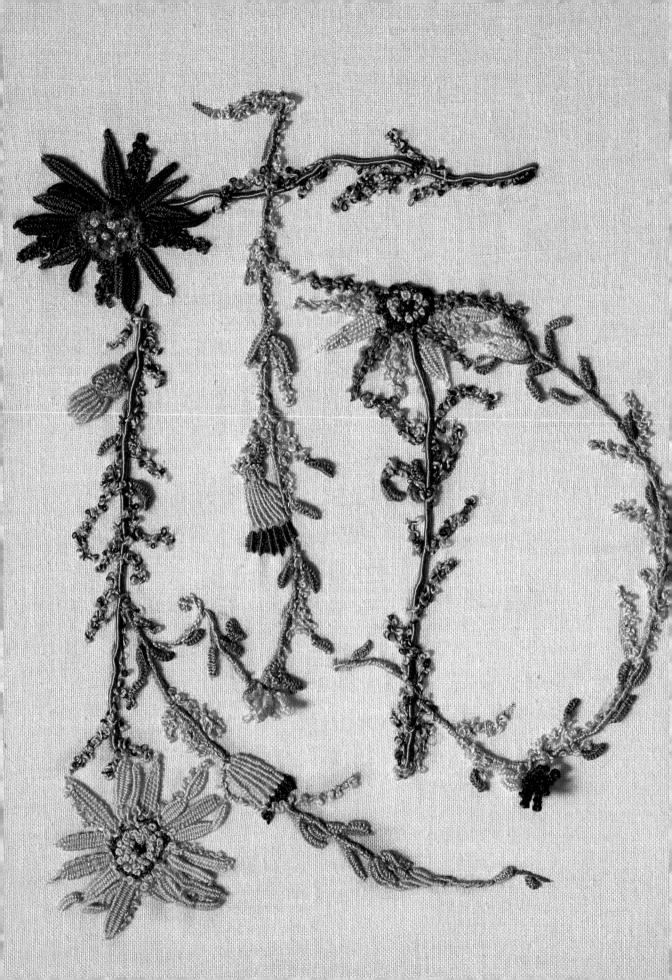

African daisy monograms

Applications: telephone book cover, scatter cushion, pillow case, garden apron pocket

The vivid colours of the simple African daisy lend themselves to varied interpretation in textured threads. This design can be used as a single daisy or translated into an entire alphabet and the art of the design is the fun factor. Choose your own alphabet and initials. Once you are satisfied with the basic letter shapes, add petals to create daisies, buds and leaves to suit your personal initials. Sketch different combinations onto a piece of paper before transferring the images onto the fabric. Try to balance the horizontal and vertical lines and allow the flourishes to link the letters.

Materials required
Background fabric (cotton, linen) and
Muslin (foundation fabric) if a ready-made pillow case is not used
Needles
Chenille no 18-22
Straw no 7/8
Textured threads
Bouclé: lime green, apricot, salmon, rust, yellow and evergreen
Yarn: lime, apricot, salmon, rust, burgundy, hunter green, yellow, evergreen
Rayon cord (round): evergreen
Chenille: salmon
Miscellaneous
3 tiny plum beads

Instructions

Draw the letters you need for your own monogram onto the background fabric. Use the shapes on page 151 as a guide. Prepare the fabric for embroidery if applicable.

1 **Stems:** We suggest two options:
   a. Round rayon cord, couched into position with matching thread (evergreen yarn or invisible thread).
   b. Overcast stem in evergreen and lime yarn.
2 **Soft leaves:** Evergreen and lime bouclé, couched around the main stem in matching yarn.
3 **Small leaves and calyxes:** Cast-on and double-sided cast-on buttonhole in evergreen, lime and hunter green yarn.
4 **Small buds:** Bullions in salmon and yellow yarn.
5 **Half open buds:** Vertical spider's web, changing colour from burgundy to apricot, yellow and salmon yarn.
6 **Spent flowers:** Drizzle stitch in burgundy and lime green yarn.
7 **Daisy:** 8-10 petals of picots and couched bouclé in shades of yellow, apricot, salmon and burgundy yarn. The picots can be woven (3 spokes) or looped (2 spokes). The spent (wrinkled) petals are bouclé couched in matching yarn.
8 **Daisy centre:** Choice of colonial knots, chenille and bouclé combining colours that are complimentary to the petals. A small burgundy bead can be used in the centre of the flower for a dash of fun.

Stitches used (see Stitch glossary page 134)
Bullion, cast-on buttonhole, double-sided cast-on buttonhole, couching, colonial knots, drizzle stitch, overcast stem, 3-spoke woven picot, 2-spoke woven picot, vertical spider's web, stem stitch
Techniques used (see New dimensions page 14)
Textured threads

Hermit crab

Applications: Small scatter cushions, framed picture.

The warm coral colours of the hermit crab (*Dardanus arrosor*) make this crustacean an interesting subject for embroidery while its environment lends itself to interesting texture options. Make a set of two on small cushions – they are fairly simple and quick to create, and washable.

Materials required
Background fabric, 35x35 cm
Foundation fabric (muslin or cotton voile)
Needles
Straw no 7-13 (ideal for bullions, cast-on-buttonhole)
Crewel no 7/8 (for basic stitches)
Chenille no18-22 (ideal for creative threads)
A selection of embroidery threads
Stranded cotton (floss): coral, peach, amber, pink
Perlé no 8: two variegated pinks, orange and a variegated yellow
Textured threads
Yarn: ecru, grey, pink, orange, yellow, toffee, brown, burgundy, two shades of lilac, peach, white, oyster white
Chenille: lilac, pink, blue and coral
Bouclé: ginger and coral
Miscellaneous
Small ball of wadding
2 bugle red beads, 2 gunmetal seed beads

Instructions

Trace the design on page 152 onto your background fabric and prepare the fabric for embroidery as described on page 17. Use the photograph and the labelled sketch as your guide and refer to the stitch glossary for details.

THE SHELL

1 **Shell outline:** Complete in stem stitch or back stitch in the appropriate colour and trapunto quilt the different segments (see page 35) before the filler stitches are introduced.

2 **Circular patterns:** Colonial knot in peach and pink yarn or couch coral bouclé with matching yarn (single strand).

3 **Groove:** Colonial knot or stab stitch in toffee and ecru yarns (single strand).

4 **Shadows:** Long and short stab stitch in shades of lilac and grey yarn (single strand).

5 **Horizontal band patterns:** Bullions (eight or more twists) and cast-on buttonhole in brown, grey and ecru yarns (single strand).

6 **Filler:** Split stitch/stab stitch/satin stitch in white and ecru yarns.

UNDERSIDE OF SHELL

1 **Horizontal band patterns:** Bullions (10 or more twists) and cast-on buttonhole in brown, grey and ecru yarns (single strand).

2 **Filler:** Split stitch/stab stitch/satin stitch in white and pink yarns.

Stitches used (see Stitch glossary page 134)
Vertical spiders web, colonial knots, bullions, couching, double-sided cast-on buttonhole, semi-detached buttonhole (needle-lace), back stitch, split stitch, long and short satin stitch, stab stitch, cast-on buttonhole, stem
Techniques used (see New dimensions page 14)
Textured threads, trapunto

SHELL UPPER

1 **Shell ridge:** Bullions (10 or more twists) in pink yarn or pink chenille couched using matching yarn or coral floss (single strand).

2 **Hairy shell (overgrown):** Couched grey/blue or lilac yarn in matching floss.

3 **Shadows:** Long and short satin stitch in shades of lilac and grey yarn (single strand).

4 **Scallops:** Bullions/stab stitch/split stitch in ecru floss (single and 2 strands).

5 **Shell curl:** Split stitch in ecru floss, variegated pink and yellow perlé and toffee yarn (single and double strands).

THE CRAB

1 **Outline:** Back stitch around the body shapes needing padding (the nippers) in orange yarn (single strand). Trapunto the body parts to create a slightly raised effect (see page 35).

2 **Nippers:** Trapunto overworked with needle-lace (semi detached buttonhole) in yellow and orange yarn or orange perlé.

3 **Nipper Detail:** Bullions (15 or more twists) and overcast stem stitch in orange yarn or coral floss.

4 **Walking legs:** Double-sided cast-on buttonhole in yellow and orange yarns.

5 **Last joints:** Bullions (10 or more twists) in yellow and orange yarn.

6 **Thorax:** Couched ginger boulé with matching thread.

7 **Antennae and tiny legs:** Bullions (15 or more twists) in apricot, amber and coral floss (2 strands).

8 **Mouth parts:** Bullions (15 or more twists) in apricot, amber and coral floss 2 strands).

9 **Eyes:** Red bugle beads with gunmetal seed beads at the top.

CORAL

Coral stitch in peach and pink perlé/yarns. Couch coral chenille and boulé with matching thread and vertical spider's web using peach and coral floss (2 strands).

brown

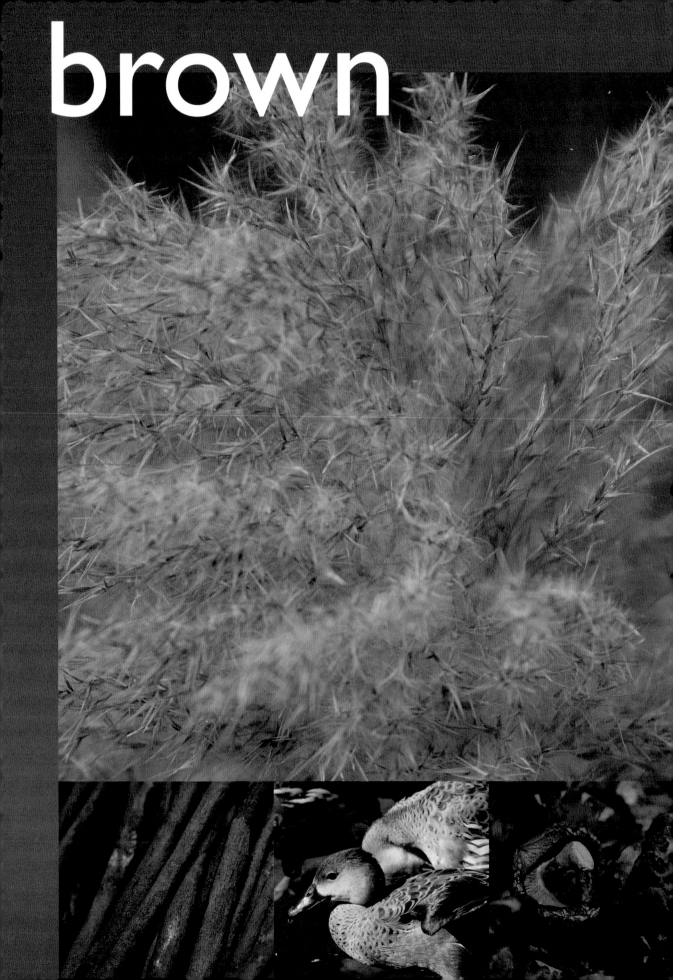

Ruffled feathers

Application: Framed picture

These barred owlets (*Glaucidium capense*) belong to what is probably the least common owl species in the Southern African region – there is a small, isolated population of barred owls in the Eastern Cape Coast region.

Materials required

Background fabric (cotton or linen), 35x35 cm

Muslin (foundation fabric)

Scraps of green and brown hand-dyed cotton fabric for appliqué

Needles

Straw no 7/8, chenille no 22, fine bead needle

A selection of embroidery threads

Stranded cotton (floss): Shades of green, yellow, mink, off white, brown, grey

Textured threads:

Yarn: black, grey, white, shades of brown, ecru, yellow, shades of green

Bouclé: off-white, mink, mottled brown, ginger

Chenille: white, off white, mink, toffee, brown

Kintted rayon cord: ginger, off-white

Wool: Shaggy variegated white/mink/brown; fringe variegated white/mink/ginger/brown; mohair brown

Ribbon

Organza: brown, white, oyster beige 6 mm wide

Miscellaneous

3 small washers

1 plastic curtain ring

Small piece of green felt

Appliqué paper/Vilene

Green stumpwork wire

Tiny black and brown beads

Tree bark

Knitting needles (6,5 mm)

The owlets are a clever manipulation of textured threads Their heads and backs are barred (striped) and this effect is translated in couched bouclé and mohair, with wonderful attention to detail in the eyes and beak. The bodies are different yet similar, an effect achieved with colour grading and shading in 'crazy' wool.

HINT

The background fabric can be painted (see page 12) before you beging your embroidery.

Instructions

Transfer the design on page 153 onto your background fabric and prepare the fabric for embroidery as described on page 17. Use the photograph as a guide and consult the stitch glossary if necessary.

PROFILE OWLET

1   **Head:** Couch bouclé, changing colour from ecru to mink and mottled brown. Soften with coiled brown mohair couched between the bouclé.

2   **Eye:** Cover 1 small washer and 1 round curtain ring with buttonhole in yellow and grey yarn. The pupil is made up of black colonial knots with one white colonial knot highlight. Stab stitch in off-white yarn between the eye and the beak.

3   **Beak:** Cut a small triangle of felt the shape of the beak and split stitch over the felt in pale grey floss (2 strands). Highlight the tip with a few yellow stab stitches (single strand).

4   **Shoulders:** Couch chenille thread in bands of mink, brown and white with matching thread (yarn of floss single strand).

Stitches used (see Stitch glossary page 134)

Couching, buttonhole, colonial knots, stab stitch, split stitch, bullion, slip stitch, seeding, semi-detached buttonhole (needlelace), stem stitch, overcast stem

Techniques used (see New dimensions page 14)

Textured threads, photo transfer, appliqué, elevated shapes, felt

5   **Small wing:** Stab stitch, brown organza ribbon.

6   **Belly fluff:** Couch fringed wool, controlling the colours to create the effect of the stripes. Stitch with matching thread in single strand or use sewing machine thread.

7   **Claws:** Couch, off-white chenille, ending with a loop through which a light grey bullion passes onto the background forming the nail (2 strands floss).

FULL FACE OWLET

1   **Head:** Couch ginger, mottled brown and ecru bouclé, controlling the shading to create the illusion of stripes and the zones around the eyes.

2   **Eyes:** Each eye, 1 washer covered with buttonhole in yellow yarn. The outer rim of the eye is single-sided-cast-on buttonhole in grey yarn. The pupil is a small dark brown/black bead held in place with white floss (single strand), to give the highlight in the eye.

3   **Beak:** Cut a small dark green triangle of felt for the beak and split stitch in pale grey and yellow floss (single and 2 strands). Stitch a brown bullion bar across the bridge of the beak and a colonial knot each side in brown and pale grey floss (single strand).

4   **Shoulders:** Unravel a piece of ginger and ecru knitted ribbon to create interesting coils. Re-arrange these coils and couch through the tube of the coils creating a soft "barred" (striped effect).

5   **Small wings:** Stab stitch brown and oyster organza ribbon. Control and shade with couched ecru bouclé.

6   **Fluffy belly:** Couch or knit a piece of shaggy wool (white, beige and brown) into the shape of the belly. Cast on and off for a more interesting shape. Trim the belly to suite the owlet, keeping the shaggy bits longer in the centre. Work a few stab stitches in triangular shapes to suggest feathers to hold it in place. Slip stitch the rest of the shape using invisible stitches.

7   **Claws:** Couch ecru chenille in horizontal bands, leaving a loop at the end. Pass a light grey bullion through the loop and onto the background (2 shades, 13-15 wraps).

8   **Bark:** The bark background is appliquéd fabric (see page 23). Attach the basic shape onto the background with buttonhole in matching thread. Embellish with real bark using tiny stab stitches (seeding) to hold it in place.

9   **Leaves:** Appliqué olive green mottled (batik-dyed) cotton onto the background using overcast stem stitch veins to secure the shapes. The edges can be left raw for a more gentle effect or they can be buttonholed in matching floss (single strand)

10 **Three-dimensional leaves:** Elevated shapes worked on a wire (see page 36). Form the shapes and needle-lace the fill with semi-detached buttonhole in evergreen yarn. Push the wired shapes into the background on completion and secure at the back.

Bouclé beetle

Application: cards, cushions, jeans pockets

Play with the dynamic contrast and the tactile quality of bouclé, rayon and yarn. The techniques are simple; couching and a few traditional crewel stitches combined with a freedom of spirit and a fun-filled approach to traditional stitchery.

Materials required
Background fabric (damask, cotton/ linen or silk)
Cotton voile (foundation fabric)
Needles
Straw no 7/8
Chenille 18 for ribbon work
Bead needle
A selection of embroidery thread
Stranded cotton (floss): apricot, brown, ginger
Textured threads
Bouclé: ginger-brown, apricot, brown
Rayon round cord: brown
Yarn: brown, apricot
Ribbon
Organza: evergreen, 6 mm wide
Miscellaneous
Tiny brown beads

Instructions

Transfer the design on page 152 onto your background fabric and prepare the fabric for embroidery as detailed on page 17. Study the photograph and the stitch glossary and enjoy a creative mixed-media experience.

1 **Head:** Brown bouclé, couched into position with matching yarn/floss (single strand)
2 **Eyes:** Tiny brown beads
3 **Feelers:** Colonial knots and bullion, brown floss (single strand).
4 **Thorax:** Brown round rayon cord outline with couched brown bouclé.
5 **Abdomen:** Brown, round rayon cord outline couched in a figure of eight rhythm. The fewer cuts in the cord, the better. Fill with apricot and ginger brown bouclé couched in place with matching yarn/floss (single strand).
6 **Wings:** Stab stitch, evergreen organza ribbon.
7 **Legs:** Cast-on buttonhole, bullion and fly stitch, in shades of ginger brown and apricot floss (single and 2 strands).

Stitches used (see Stitch glossary page 134)
Bullions, cast-on buttonhole, couching, fly stitch, stab stitch, colonial knots
Techniques Used (see New dimensions page 14)
Textured threads, beads

pink

inspiration

projects

Heather

Application: Framed picture

Also known as black-eyed heather, *Erica canaliculata* bears masses of small pink flowers with dark maroon centres in summer. This glorious shrub is an important fynbos species. It grows on the Southern Cape seaboard of South Africa and is prolific between Knysna and Plettenberg Bay. It lends itself to interesting interpretation in free-style stitchery and creative threads.

Materials required
Background fabric (cotton, linen or silk), 50x60 cm
Muslin or cotton voile (foundation fabric)
Needles
Straw no 7/8
Chenille no 18/22 (for cord work)
A selection of embroidery threads
Stranded cotton (floss): shades of pink (light pink rose pink, lilac pink) burgundy, brown, khaki green
Perlé: variegated avocado/olive, variegated blue/green, variegated lilac/pink, burgundy
Textured threads
Yarn: evergreen, hunter green, brown
Bouclé: evergreen, mottled green, hunter green, mottled pink
Rayon cord (round): brown

Instructions

Transfer the design on page 154 to the background fabric and prepare the fabric for embroidery as detailed on page 17. Study the photograph and the stitch glossary and enjoy a creative mixed-media experience.

1 **Main stems:** Brown, round rayon cord couched in position with matching brown yarn/floss (single strand).

2 **Fine stems:** stem stitch, brown and green yarn/floss (single and 2 strands).

3 **Fine leaves:** fly stitch and romanian, shades of green yarn/floss (avocado, khaki, blue/green, single and 2 strands) and khaki green perlé.

4 **Course leaves:** extended fly, mottled green and hunter green bouclé.

5 **Tiny buds:** colonial knots, light pink, rose pink and lilac pink floss or perlé (single and 2 strands).

6 **Small profile buds:** a combination of colonial knots, lazy daisy &stab stitch, in burgundy, light pink floss and perlé (single and 2 strands).

7 **Plump profile buds:** colonial knots, bullion and stab stitch, combination in lilac/pink perlé/floss (single and 2 strands) and burgundy perlé /floss (single and 2 strands).

8 **Full blown blooms:** Colonial knots in burgundy perlé/floss (single and 2 strands) with a bullion surround in pale pink and lilac pink perlé /floss (single strand).

9 **Background blooms:** Mottled pink bouclé couched in position with matching yarn/floss (single strand).

Stitches used (see Stitch glossary page 134)
Stem stitch, stab stitch, fly stitch, extended fly stitch, Romanian, detached chain (lazy daisy), bullion knot, colonial knot, couching
Techniques (see New dimensions page 14)
Textured threads

Fragile fynbos

Application: Miniature cushions, neck cushion, tray inset, guest towels

Fynbos refers to a biome stretching from the West coast to the Southern Cape in South Africa, as well as the diverse group of small, fine-leaved plants which grow there. The diversity of plants is huge and this combination of erica, glossy currant, blombos and pelargonium represents but a tiny sample of the more than 9 000 species. Combine floss, perlé and silk-ribbon to create this delightful scene of some of the smallest of the world's floral kingdom.

Materials required
Fabric (linen, cotton or silk) 30x30 cm
Muslin (foundation fabric)
Needles
Chenille no 22
Straw no 8/9
A selection of embroidery threads
Stranded cotton (floss): shades of green, brown, burgundy, plum, ochre
Perlé (in variegated shades): variegated plum, shades of olive green, light and dark pink, white
Ribbon
Silk ribbon: rose, pale pink, green (3,5 mm wide)

Instructions

Transfer the design on page 155 onto the background fabric and prepare the fabric for embroidery as detailed on page 17. Study the labelled template and refer to the stitch glossary as a guide.

ERICA

1. **Bloom:** Bullion, colonial knot, light and dark pink perlé.
2. **Stamens:** Stab stitch, burgundy floss (single strand).
3. **Leaves:** Fly and feather stitch, blue/green floss.
4. **Stem:** Stem stitch, brown floss (single strand).

GLOSSY CURRANT

1. **Berries:** Colonial knots, plum variegated perlé
2. **Leaves:** Romanian, shades of olive green, perlé and floss (single and double strands).

BLOMBOS

1. **Bloom:** Lazy daisy, white perlé and pink floss (single strand) with fly stitch outline, plum floss (single strand).
2. **Bud:** Extended French knots, colonial knots and fly stitch, white perlé with plum floss outline (single strand).
3. **Tiny stalks:** Bullion, ochre floss (single strand).
4. **Calyx:** Bullion, blue/green floss (single strand).
5. **Leaves:** Bullion, blue/green floss (2 strands)

PELARGONIUM

1. **Bud:** Cast-on buttonhole, avocado green floss (single strand).
2. **Blooms:** Stab stitch, rose and pale pink ribbon with stab stitch, old rose and plum rose detail (single strand).
3. **Stems:** Overcast stem stitch, avocado green floss (2 strands).
4. **Calyx:** Lazy daisy, avocado green floss (2 strands).
5. **Leaves:** Ruched green silk ribbon.
6. **Sand:** Stab stitch, brown floss (single strand).

Stitches used (see Stitch glossary page 134)
Stab stitch, bullion, French knot, extended French knots, back stitch, buttonhole, fly stitch, Romanian, feather stitch, basic bullion knot and rosebud, chain stitch, detached chain (lazy daisy), stem stitch, over-cast stem, colonial knot, cast-on buttonhole
Techniques used (see New dimensions page 14)
Ribbon techniques (fluted/ruched petals)

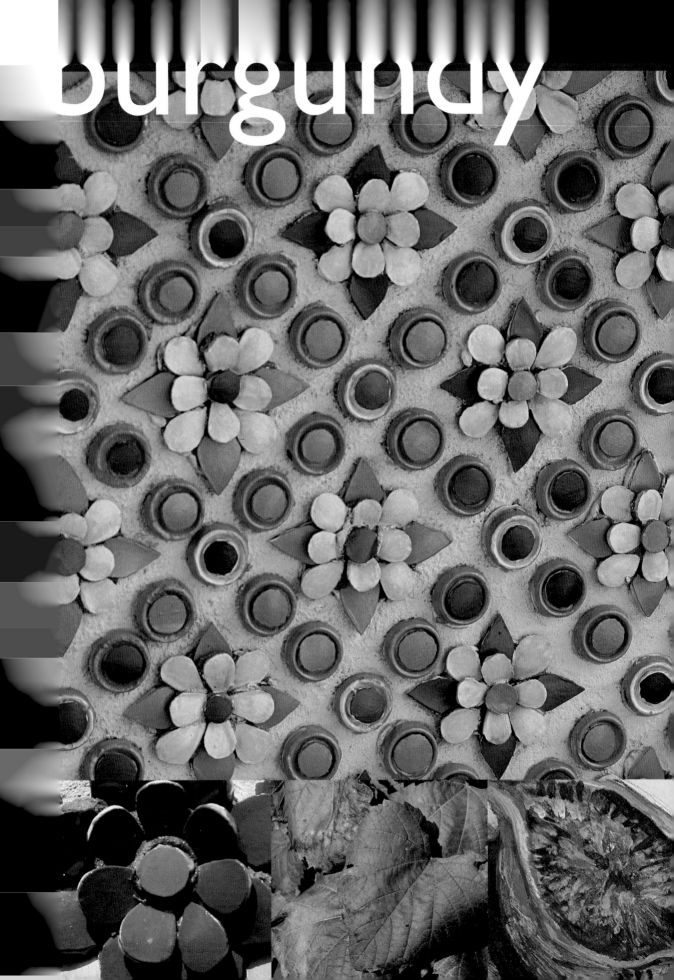

burgundy

inspiration

projects

Burgundy passion flower

Application: Framed picture, soft funishings

The exotic complexity of the burgundy passion flower (*Passiflora incarnata*) bloom lends itself to exciting interpretations in textured thread and ribbon.

Materials required
Fabric (silk dupion, cotton and linen) 40x50 cm
Muslin (foundation fabric)
Small pieces of peach and burgundy silk/taffeta for appliqué

Needles
Chenille no 18-22
Straw no 7/8

A selection of embroidery threads
Stranded cotton (floss): shades of green, pink, peach, burgundy, yellow, khaki, brown
Perlé (in variegated shades): green

Textured threads:
Bouclé: evergreen
Chenille: evergreen, burgundy/indigo
Yarn: evergreen, burgundy/indigo
Round rayon cord: brown
Fringed wool in white and burgundy (15 mm wide)

Ribbon
Organza: light-dark burgundy 15 mm wide
Taffeta: rich olive green 25 mm wide

Miscellaneous
Appliqué paper
Green wire for tendrils
1 plastic curtain ring for centre
3 round beads for pistils

Instructions

Transfer the design on page 156 to the background fabric and prepare the fabric for embroidery as described on page 17. Use the photograph of the embroidered design as a guide and refer to the stitch glossary and the techniques for finer details.

1 **Small bud:** Split or stab stitch, plum/old rose floss (single strand).

2 **Small leaf:** Romanian, avocado green and olive floss (single strand).

3 **Flat tendril:** Chain stitch, variegated olive green floss or yarn (single strand).

4 **Calyx:** Silk/taffeta ribbon appliqué (see page 23), buttonhole edge in olive green floss (single strand).
   Leaf curl: Cast-on buttonhole, olive green floss (single strand).
   Veins: Fine chain, olive green floss (single strand).

5 **Large bud:** Silk/taffeta appliqué, split stitch details in plum/old rose and peach floss (single strand).
   Vein: Overcast stem stitch, mustard/ yellow floss or yarn (single and 2 strands).

6 **Textured leaf:** Couched, green chenille and mottled green bouclé. Outline in stem stitch or chain, olive green variegated perlé or yarn.
   Vein: Couched brown, round rayon cord.

7 **Wired tendril:** See technique page 31. Buttonhole, olive green floss on wire (single strand).

8 **Large leaf:** Ruched olive green taffeta ribbon or fabric (see page 43).
   Leaf vein: Couched, brown rayon cord.

9 **Stalk:** Stem stitch, variegated olive green perlé.

Stitches used (see Stitch glossary page 134)
Stab stitch, stem stitch, chain stitch, split stitch, romanian, couching, basic bullion knot, rosebud, buttonhole, cast-on buttonhole, double-sided cast-on buttonhole, overcast stem, gathering

Techniques used (see New dimensions page 14)
Textured threads, elevated shapes, silk/taffeta appliqué, ribbon work, wrapped beads

10 **Bloom:**

Large calyx petal: Burgundy silk/taffeta appliqué (see page 23) edged with matching buttonhole floss/yarn (single strand).

Soft petal: Stab stitch, light and dark plum, organdy ribbon with split stitch, details plum floss/yarn (single strand).

11 **Pistil:** Three beads wrapped (see page 45) with plum floss (single strand).

Stem: Bullion in plum floss/yarn (single strand).

Centre: Bullion rosebud in variegated olive green floss (two strands).

Extensions: Cast-on buttonhole and double sided cast-on buttonhole in variegated olive green floss (single strand).

12 **Filaments:** Gathered organza ribbon (see page 18) in burgundy and white or silky fringe. Anchor the ribbon with burgundy chenille or a plastic ring, buttonholed with burgundy floss, (single strand). The organza ribbon can be frayed by cutting the outer edge and separating the warp from the weft with a pin. The outer edge is then quickly seared with a flame to create tiny balls on the edge of the ribbon.

African grasshopper

Application: framed picture, drinks-tray inset

The multi-coloured African grasshopper (*Zonocerus variegatus*), also known as the variegated grasshopper, occurs throughout the African continent. It offers much scope for the use of textured threads in free-style embroidery.

Materials required
China silk (dyed, painted or photo transfer)
Background fabric (cotton, damask, linen)
Muslin (foundation fabric)

Needles
Straw no 7/8, crewel no 7/8, chenille no 22

A selection of embroidery thread
Stranded cotton/yarn: yellow, black, apricot, ginger, brown, shades of green
Metallic thread: black/gold

Textured thread
Chenille: yellow
Rayon cord (round): yellow

Ribbon
Organza: olive green (15 mm widw)

Miscellaneous
Blue/black bead
Rayon cord
Appliqué paper

Instructions

Photo transfer the embroidered design, or lightly sketch the design on page 157 onto the background fabric and prepare the fabric for embroidery as described on page 17. Prepare appliqué shapes as described on page 23.

1. Once appliqué shapes are ironed onto the background fabric, begin by buttonhole stitching the raw edges of the silk appliqué in matching tones of floss (single strand). The shapes are now ready for fine embroidery details.
2. **Wings:** Make a stab stitch with green organza ribbon, creating an illusion of a fine wing. Couch the veins on the wing in shades of green yarn.
3. **Abdomen:** Couch the abdomen in yellow chenille with holding stitches of brown bullions (single strand).
4. **Thorax:** The helmet-like area is overcast stem, colonial knots and bullions in black, yellow and ginger floss (single strand).
5. **Head:** Colonial knots, in yellow, black and ginger floss (single strand).
6. **Eye:** blue/black bead attached with yellow floss.
7. **Feelers:** Stem stitch, black/gold metallic floss (half strand).
8. **Large upper back leg:** Overcast stem outline (or rayon cord) in yellow and green floss (single and 2 strands) with a filler of bullion and colonial knots, yellow, black and rust floss (single strand).
9. **Middle section of legs:** Double-sided cast-on buttonhole, yellow and black floss (single strand).
10. **Lower leg section:** Bullions, yellow and black floss (single strand) ending in fly stitch.

Stitches used (see Stitch glossary page 134)
Stem stitch, overcast stem, stab stitch, bullion knot, colonial knot, buttonhole, cast-on buttonhole, double-sided cast-on buttonhole, fly stitch, couching

Techniques used (see New dimensions page 14)
Textured threads, photo transfer, silk appliqué, ribbon techniques

Grasshopper in motion

Application: framed picture, inset in a drinks tray

The challenge of this insect is the interpretation in threads and ribbons of the ungainly body balanced by the delicate wings.

Materials required
Background fabric: linen 30x30 cm
Muslin (foundation fabric)
Needles
Straw no 7/8
Chenille no 18
A selection of embriodery threads
Stranded cotton (floss): cherry red floss, black, yellow, grey, indigo, burgundy, plum, lilac
Bouclé: blue (optional)
Metallic thread: gold, silver/black
Ribbon
Organza: yellow (6 mm wide)
light blue (15 mm wid)
Miscellaneous
Blue snake-skin or soft leather (hand-dyed)

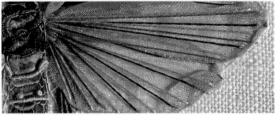

Instructions

Photo transfer the embroidered design, or lightly sketc the design on page 157 onto the background fabric and prepare the fabric for embroidery as described on page 17. Use the photograph of the embroidered grasshopper as a guide.

1 **Feelers:** Stem stitch, metallic black/silver thread (single strand)

2 **Head:** Padded cherry red floss, satin stitch (single strand). The neck extension is a combination of tiny bullions and colonial knots in bright yellow and black floss (single strand).

3 **Thorax and abdomen (body):** Appliqué a small piece of dyed blue snake-skin (or soft leather) onto the background (see technique on page 23). Couched blue bouclé is an excellent substitute. Embellish the surface and adhere the shape with grey cast-on buttonhole and bullions (single strand) floss for the thorax area. Decorate the abdomen with colonial knots and bullions in shades of yellow floss (single strand) with a central delineation in gold metallic thread in stab stitch.

4 **Front legs:** Work long, vertical bullions in black floss (single strand) and satin stitch yellow floss over the bullions approximately a match head apart. At the elbow joint change to small black and yellow bullions, in a horizontal direction (single strand floss). Change back to vertical yellow and black bullions and end with a lazy daisy, fly stitch and colonial knot (claw/tip).

5 **Hind legs:** Begin at the wing/thorax edge with grey and yellow bullions in floss (single strand). Alternate the colours and change from vertical to horizontal along the leg to suit the design. Change to yellow

Stitches used (see Stitch glossary page 134)
Stem stitch, padded satin stitch, colonial knot bullions, cast-on buttonhole, stab stitch, bullions, satin stitch, lazy daisy, fly stitch, buttonhole, vertical spider's web, couching
Techniques used (see New dimensions page 14)
Appliqué, ribbon work, photo transfer

and black fly stitch (single strand floss) half way down the leg. End with colonial knots and bullions in yellow and black floss (single strand).

6   **Upper wings:** Make one long stab stitch in yellow organza ribbon. Manipulate the ribbon and embellish with long and short stab stitch in indigo and light grey floss (single strand). For more control, the outline of the ribbon can be buttonhole stitched in yellow floss (single strand).

7   **Lower wings:** Make two long stab stitches per side in light blue organza ribbon 15mm wide. Manipulate the ribbon to acquire a wing shape and embellish with very long stab stitches in alternating burgundy and light lilac floss (single strand).

8   **Lower left wing:** Work stab stitches in vertical spider's web starting near the thorax with plum coloured floss (single strand). Work towards the outer wing increasing the space and shade from plum to light lilac. Stitch matching wings for a fine skeletal effect or leave one wing slightly different (as shown on the photograph) to hint at the the delicate pleating of the wing as it unfolds.

indigo

inspiration

projects

Forbidden fruit

Application: Decorative arrangement

Embroidered three-dimensional shapes in felt are a fabulously innovative concept for interior decoration. Make a collection of three-dimensional forbidden fruit in fibre and thread that will last indefinitely. Pop it into a hand-painted bowl and use as a table decoration in the dining room or kitchen. Start with this three-dimensional fig.

Materials required
Hand-dyed felt, cream, indigo
Needles
Long straw needle and bead needle no 1 and 7/8
A selection of embroidery threads
Yarns/floss: yellow, pink, plum, burnt orange, brown, indigo, dark lilac, burgundy, light lilac, olive green, evergreen
Miscellaneous
Pearly pink and yellow beads
Green round rayon cord
Wadding

Instructions

Use the template on page 159 and trace the fig sections onto the felt (five segments in purple for the closed fig, three segments in purple, one in cream for the cut fig). Use the photograph as a guide.

CLOSED FIG

1 Back stitch the five shapes together starting from the base to the stalk. Do not close up the last two sides. This opening allows you to hold the shape and to create the shading.

2 **Shading:** Working in split stitch, start with brown embroidery thread at the base, and change colours in the following order: dark lilac, indigo, burgundy, olive green and ending with evergreen at the top. Keep the stitches short and regular. At the base of the fig, make a yellow star-like pattern in stab stitch using yellow yarn.

3 **Final construction:** After shading the fig, turn it inside out and join the last two sides, leaving a small opening at the top and turn through. Push wadding into the open shape (fuller at the base and softer towards the stalk). Slip hem the last seam closed stopping 1cm short of the top.

4 **The stalk:** Fold 6 cm of green round rayon cord in half to make a small loop. Push the raw ends into the neck of the fig shape and make a few back stitches in evergreen yarn/floss to secure the loop. Pinch the halves together to become one and wrap the thread around it. Separate again and wrap into a loop 5 mm from the top. To end off, push the needle down the shaft between the wrapped halves. End at the base of the stalk with an invisible back stitch or two..

5 Add further subtle shading to the basic fig shape to camouflage any joins.

Stitches used (see Stitch glossary page 134)
Slip hemming, split stitch, bullions, back stitch
Techniques used (see New dimensions page 14)
Felt work, beading

CUT FIG

1   Back stitch the three purple segments together and shade as for the closed fig.
2   Embroider the flesh on the cream section with long and short bullions in apricot, yellow, plum and pink floss (single strand) with pearly pink beads as pip detail.
3   **The pith:** Seeding, ecru floss/yarn on the cream felt (single strand).
4   **To join:** With right sides together, back stitch the transverse section to the outer skin leaving a small opening at the base. Trim and clip seams and turn through. Push polyester wadding into the cavity and slip hem the opening closed. Extra subtle shading can be added to the basic fig shape to camouflage any joins.
5   **The stalk stump:** Select a subtle green and run a gathering thread around the neck of the fig, pulling it very tight to create the illusion of a plucked stump. If it looks good leave it, otherwise work some green stitches into the tiny plucked end.

Butterfly and ladybird

Application: dinner mats, serviettes, scatter cushions and floral pictures

Butterflies and bugs can be interpreted in a myriad different ways. Enjoy a voyage of discovery with organza ribbon and textured threads for this rendition. Play with the dynamic contrast of sheer organza and the tactile quality of chenille, bouclé, rayon and yarn. The techniques are simple: couching and a few traditional crewel stitches combined with a freedom of spirit and a fun-filled approach to traditional stitchery.

Materials required
Damask background fabric (cotton/linen or silk)
Cotton voile (foundation fabric)

Needles
Straw no 7/8
Chenille no 18 for ribbon work
Bead needle no 9/10

A selection of embroidery thread
Metallic thread: antique silver/black, antique gold/black.

Textured thread
Chenille: brown, indigo, lilac
Bouclé: red, apricot
Knitted rayon cord (flat): ginger
Floss/yarn: apricot, ochre, shades of purple, teal, brown, black, red

Ribbon
Organza: ochre (6 mm wide)

Miscellaneous
Tiny burgundy/brown beads

Instructions

Transfer the design on page 157 to the background fabric and prepare the fabric for embroidery as detailed on page 17. These instructions are for a life-size butterfly.

LADYBIRD

1 **Body:** Mottled red bouclé couched in matching yarn/floss (single strand).
2 **Head:** Bullion rosebud, black floss (single strand).
3 **Feelers:** Extended French knots, antique silver/black metallic thread (half strand).
4 **Legs:** Backstitch, antique silver/black metallic thread (half strand).

BUTTERFLY

1 **Head and eye:** Bullion, brown floss (single strand) with tiny burgundy/brown beads.
2 **Feelers:** Stem stitch and bullion tips, antique silver/black metallic thread (half strand).
3 **Abdomen and thorax:** Brown chenille couched in place with matching floss (single strand) and a few bullion details.
4 **Wings:** Couched indigo and lilac chenille. Work with matching yarn where the effect is a velvet patch. Linear edges can be accented with yellow satin stitch (single strand) over the couched chenille. The ochre areas are organza ribbon, manipulated into position with couched apricot bouclé in a linear rhythm. Purple spots are purple colonial knots in 2 strands of floss.
5 **Top edge of upper wing:** Couch ginger rayon cord (flat) in place, with matching floss (single strand).
6 **Veins:** Stab stitch, teal and apricot floss (single strand).

Stitches used (see Stitch glossary page 134)
Bullions, colonial knots, couching, extended French knots, padded satin stitch, stem stitch, stab stitch, back stitch

Techniques used (see New dimensions page 14)
Textured threads

grey
black & white

inspiration

projects

Light Sussex Cock

Application: Apron pockets, dinner mats, scatter cushions, dishcloths and framed pictures

Embroider these delightful crazy chickens in a set of four or as individual pieces. Use the photograph (note the hen on the inspiration page) as a guide. The design is simple and quick to create, and washable.

Materials required
Background fabric or item to be embellished
Foundation fabric (muslin or cotton voile)
Needles
Straw no 7/8, crewel no 7/8, chenille no 18-22
A selection of embroidery threads
Stranded cotton (floss): 2 shades of pink, charcoal grey, red, white
Perlé no 12 or yarn: red, yellow
Metallic silver thread
Textured threads:
Yarn: black and charcoal
Knitted rayon cord (flat): red
Ribbon
Silk ribbon: black, white (3,5 mm wide)
Organza ribbon: white (3,5 mm wide)
Miscellaneous
Small ball of wadding

Instructions

Transfer the design on page 159 to the background fabric and prepare the fabric for embroidery as described on page 17. Use the photograph of the embroidered roosters as a guide and enjoy a crazy chicken run.

THE HEAD

1 **Cheek:** Satin Stitch in old pink and rose pink floss above and below the eye (single strand).

2 **Marking:** Colonial knot in white floss (2 strands).

3 **Eye:** Colonial knot in black yarn (single strand).

4 **Beak:** 2 bullions (6 twists) in yellow floss (single strand).

5 **Cock's comb and wattle:** Stab stitch/satin stitch in red perlé and/or red floss (single strand). Optional: add extra detail in by couching red flat rayon over the satin/stab stitches for the larger version.

THE BODY

1 Outline around the body shape, excluding head, with back stitch in charcoal floss (single strand). Stitch a second row of stem/split stitch next to back stitch in same colour. Trapunto body and tail feather section to create a slightly raised effect (see page 35). Stab stitch white organdy ribbon below wing, couch white chenille on upper back.

2 **Neck:** Stab stitch and detached chain/lazy daisy stitch in different sizes (smallest stitch starting form base of neck), charcoal and white yarn. Detail with stab stitch in metallic silver/black over detached chain/lazy daisy.

3 **Wing:** Stab stitch outline in white and black silk ribbon. Fill with couched grey chenille. Accent wing shape in stem/stab stitch, metallic silver/black thread. Optional: decorate with fly stitches in white yarn.

4 **Tail feathers:** Stab stitch in black silk ribbon. Detail with stab stitch in metallic silver/black thread..

THE FEET

1 **Legs:** Buttonhole in old pink and rose pink floss down the leg (single strand). Then outline in stem stitch using charcoal grey floss around pink buttonholes (single strand).

2 **Claws:** Fill with pink bullions (2 strands) and end with tiny charcoals grey floss bullions (single strand).

Stitches used (see Stitch glossary page 134)
Buttonhole, bullions, stab stitch, stem stitch, detached chain/lazy daisy, back stitch, satin stitch, colonial knot
Techniques used (see New dimensions page 14)
Trapunto, ribbon work

Pastel passion flower

Application: Framed picture

Also known as the blue passion flower *Passiflora caerule* is actually creamy white but the filaments are banded with blue or purple. This tendril-climbing vine is grown primarily for its exotic blooms in colours ranging from crisp white to almost black purple depending on the species. The bloom's frilly filaments and pronounced stamens make it an exciting choice for interpretations in textured thread and ribbon.

Instructions

Transfer the design on page 158 to your background fabric and prepare the fabric for embroidery as described on page 17. Use the photograph as a guide and refer to the stitch glossary and techniques section for details to enjoy a creative mixed-media experience. Choose between trapunto and appliqué for the fruit.

BUDS, LEAVES AND TENDRILS

1   **Small buds:** Bullions in lime green floss (single strand).
2   **Perlé/yarn leaves:** Chain/parma stitch, lime and evergreen.
3   **Small leaves:** We give two suggestions:
    a. Split/chain stitch in lime and evergreen floss (single strand).
    b. Romanian/buttonhole stitch, shades of green yarn.
4   **Textured leaf:** Couched chenille and bouclé (evergreen and lime combination). Outline and fill in stem stitch, green perlé or yarn.
5   **Applique leaf:** Dyed fabric (see appliqué page 23) edged with buttonhole in matching floss (single

strand). Central vein whipped chain in green yarn.

6 **Large leaf:** Ruched olive green taffeta ribbon or fabric (see technique page 43), leaf vein couched, green rayon cord.

7 **Large bud:** Cotton/taffeta appliqué (see appliqué page 23), split stitch details in shades of green yarn and floss (single strand) or couched lime chenille. Vein overcast stem stitch, lime floss or yarn (double and single strand).

8 **Flat tendril:** Chain stitch, olive green floss or yarn (single strand).

9 **Wired tendril:** Buttonhole (see technique page 31) olive green floss on wire (single strand).

FRUIT

1 **Cotton/taffeta appliqué:** Follow instructions on page 23 and iron shape into position on background fabric.

2 **Outline:** Back stitch in yellow floss. Lightly stuff the outlined area with wadding (see Trapunto page 35).

3 **Filler:** Couch bouclé, salmon, apricot and wild wheat with matching yarn and highlight with colonial knots in the same colours.

4 **Tip:** Bullion, brown floss (single strand).

5 **Spent calyx:** 3-spoke picot in evergreen yarn or perlé.

6 **Stalk:** Stem stitch, shades of green perlé or yarn.

BLOOM

1 **Ribbon petals:** Stab stitch, evergreen organdy ribbon and white silk ribbon.

2 **Wired petals:** Use stiff white organdy fabric and follow steps on page 42 to prepare. Add shading with split stitch in oyster beige floss (single strand).

3 **Pistil:** Three beads wrapped with evergreen floss (single strand) or plain beads.
   Tiny stem: Chain stitch, evergreen floss (single strand).
   Centre: Bullion rosebud in lime and moss green floss (two strands).
   Centre stalk: Double sided cast-on-buttonhole, lime green floss (two strands).
   Extensions: Bullions and lazy daisy in lime and moss green floss, (single strand).

4 **Filaments:** Couched white and variegated blue/green/purple silky fringe. Anchor the fringe with a plastic ring, buttonhole stitched in ochre floss (single strand). Fill the centre of the ring with colonial knots in indigo yarn.

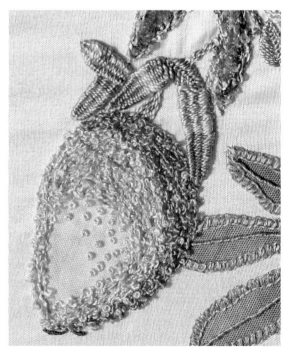

Creative Threads, packs of textured
threads, cord and ribbon, as well as
silk screens of designs featured in
this book are available from
Les Designs CC, PO Box 82
Sedgefield 6573, South Africa
Tel RSA: +27 (0) 44343 2034
    ASIA: +852 9222 8952
Fax RSA:+27 (0) 44382 0708
Email: ldesigns@mweb.co.za
thewepeners@hotmail.com

Stitches used

Outline stitches and border stitches

Stem stitch

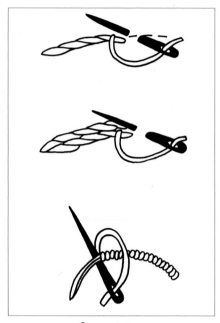

Overcast stem

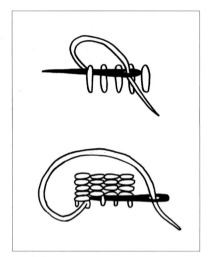

Raised stem

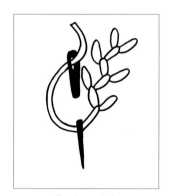

Feather stitch

Coral stitch

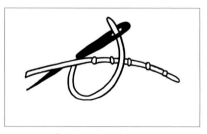

Couching/couch/baste

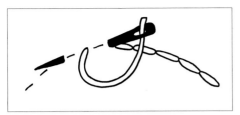

Back stitch

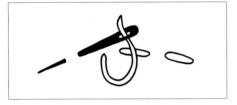

Running stitch/gathering stitch

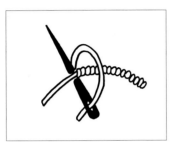

Whipping stitch/wrapping

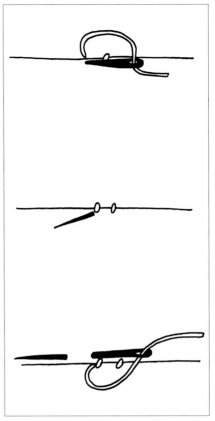

Slip stitch/hemming

Chain stitches

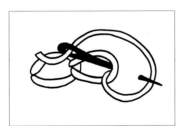

Chain stitch

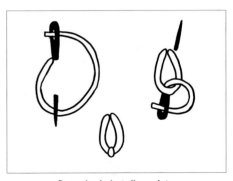

Detached chain/lazy daisy

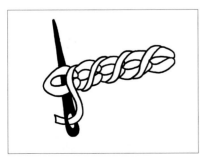

Whipped chain

Raised chain

Buttonhole stitches

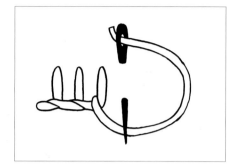

Buttonhole

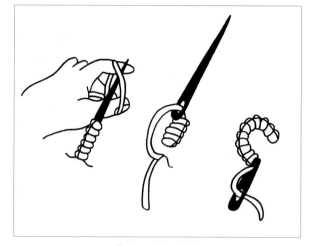

Cast-on buttonhole

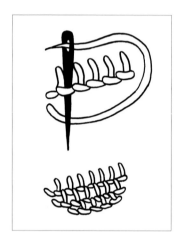

Semi-detached buttonhole
(needlelace)

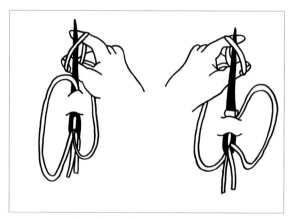

Double-sided cast-on buttonhole

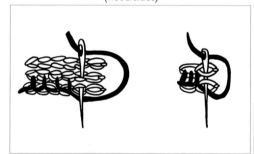

Parma stitch

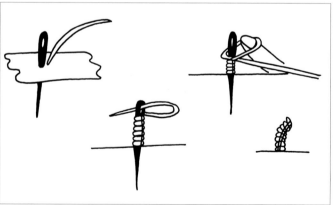

Drizzle stitch

Isolated and filling stitches

Satin stitch

Long and short satin stitch

Stab stitch

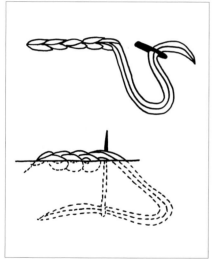

Split stitch

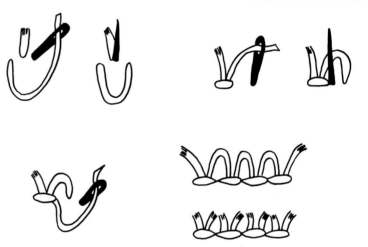

Tufting/turkey work

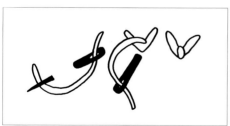

Fly stitch

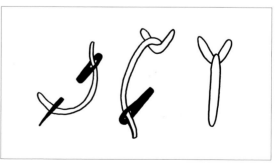

Extended fly stitch

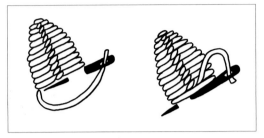

Romanian stitch

Fishbone stitch

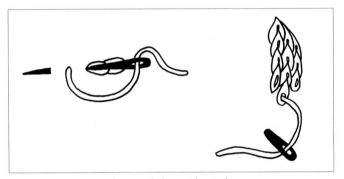

Long and short split stitch

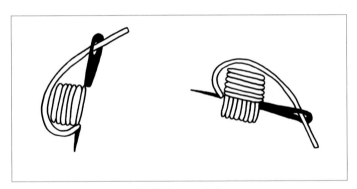

Padded satin stitch

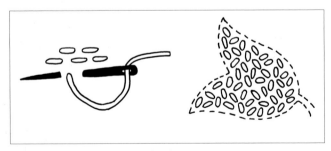

Seeding

Woven stitches

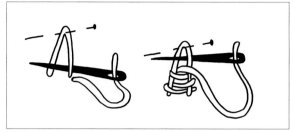

2-spoke woven picot

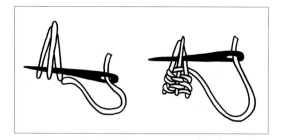

3-spoke woven picot

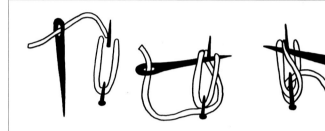

Detached woven picot

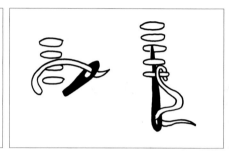

Vertical spider's web

Knot stitches

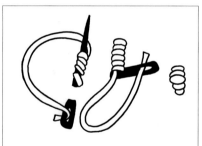

Basic bullion knot

Bullion rosebud

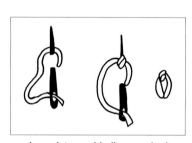

Lazy daisy and bullion rosebud

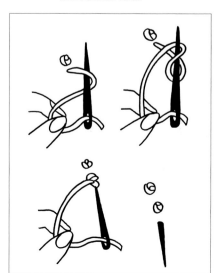

Colonial knot

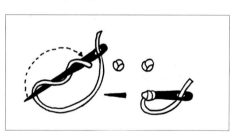

French knot

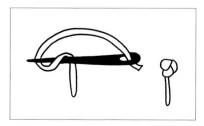

Extended French knot

139

Ribbon stitches

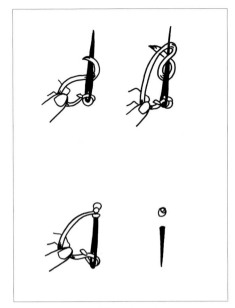

Colonial knot

Stab stitch

Looped 3-D petals

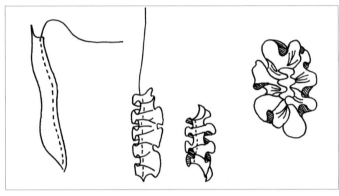

Fluted/ruched petals

Machine stitching

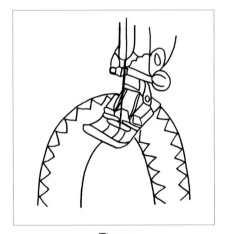

Zig-zag

Blombos

(enlarge by 100%)

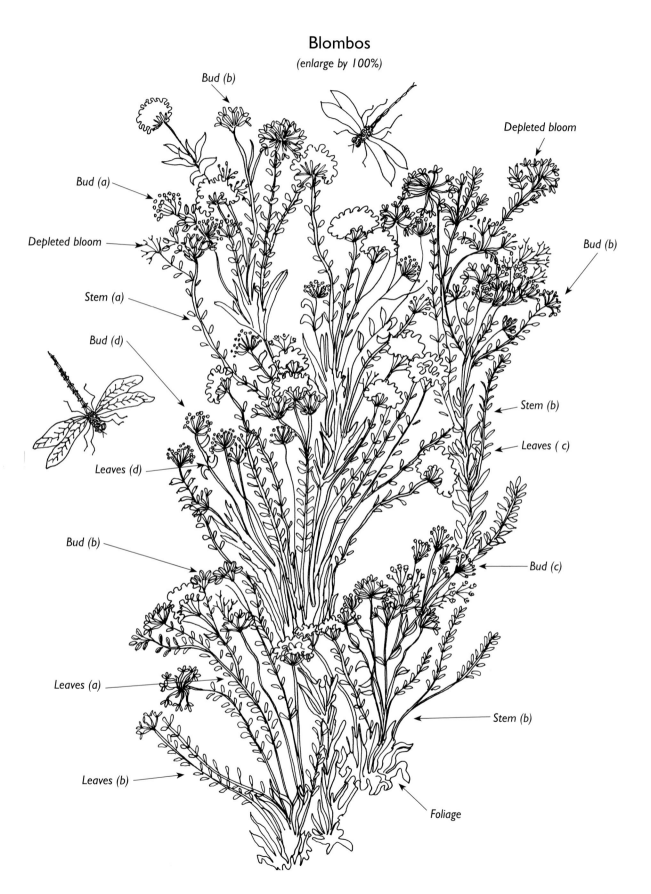

Bud (b)

Depleted bloom

Bud (a)

Depleted bloom

Stem (a)

Bud (d)

Bud (b)

Stem (b)

Leaves (c)

Leaves (d)

Bud (b)

Bud (c)

Leaves (a)

Stem (b)

Leaves (b)

Foliage

Dragonfly for PJ's or beach gear

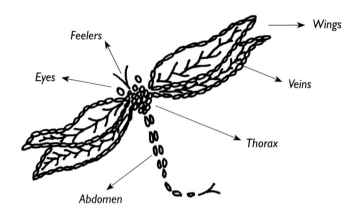

Feelers

Eyes

Wings

Veins

Thorax

Abdomen

Dragonflies

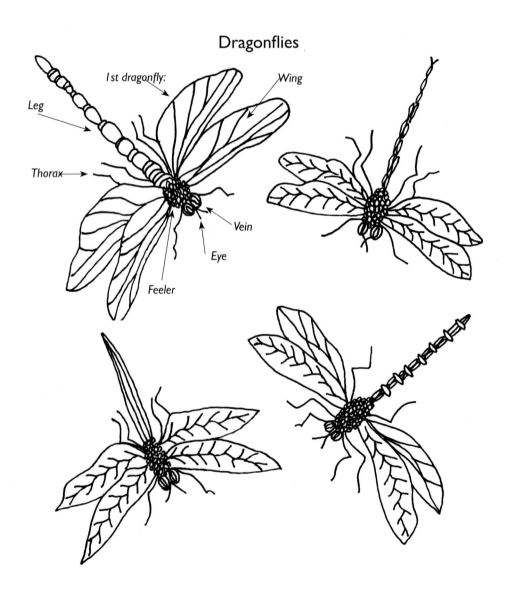

1st dragonfly:

Wing

Leg

Thorax

Vein

Eye

Feeler

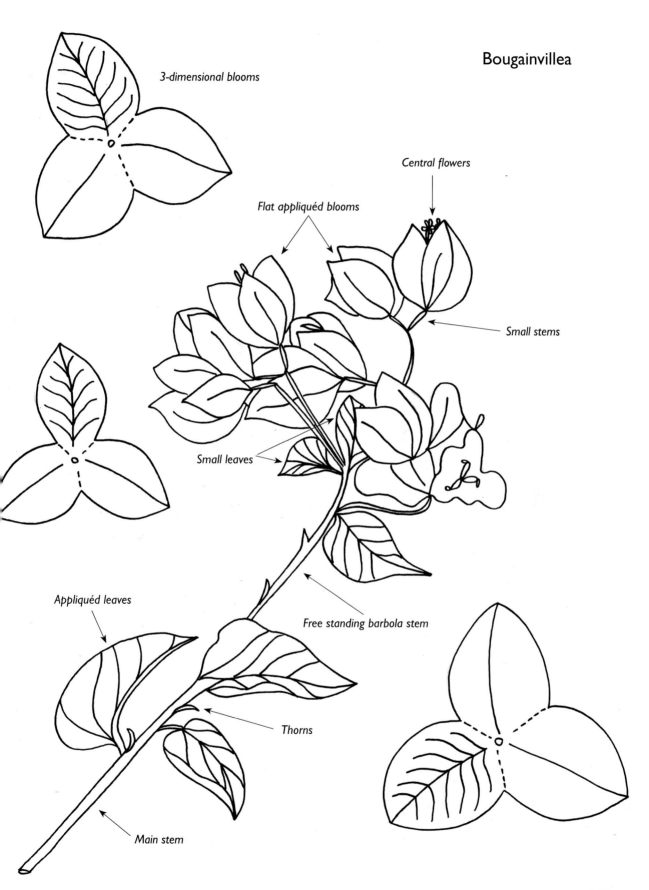

Bougainvillea

3-dimensional blooms

Central flowers

Flat appliquéd blooms

Small stems

Small leaves

Appliquéd leaves

Free standing barbola stem

Thorns

Main stem

Gerbera

(slightly smaller than actual size)

Template 1: cut 2

Template 6: draw around

Template 3: cut 1

Template 5: cut 2

Template 2: cut 1

Template 4: cut 1

Gerbera
(assembly diagrams)

Diagram a
Bend each wire in half around your finger, measure 3 cm from the bottom of the wire and twist the wire.

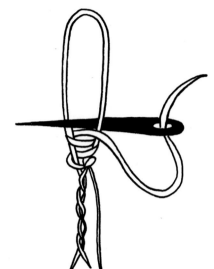

Diagram b
Using the back of a large chenille needle weave back and forth to fill the wire space.

Diagram c
Use 7mm silk ribbon in the second tow, secure with a colonial knot

Use 4mm silk ribbon in the first row close to the bouclé, secure with a colonial knot

Couch chenille in a spiral here

Couch bouclé following this pattern after the chenille

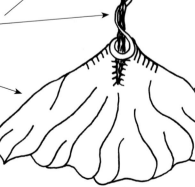

Diagram d
Green stem wire secured at the base and wrapped around the petal wires

Petal wires twisted together

Final petal over the centre

Nesting Weaver

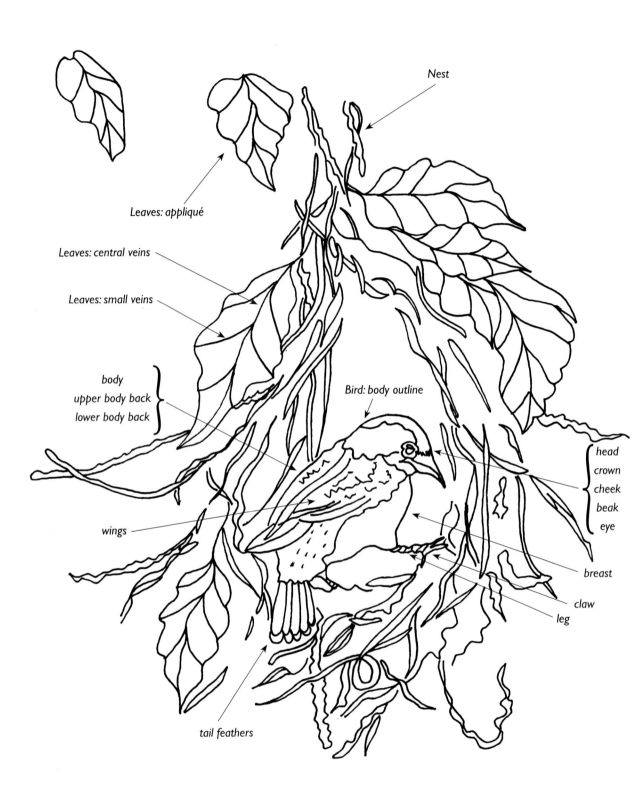

Nest

Leaves: appliqué

Leaves: central veins

Leaves: small veins

body
upper body back
lower body back

Bird: body outline

head
crown
cheek
beak
eye

wings

breast

claw

leg

tail feathers

The Mantids

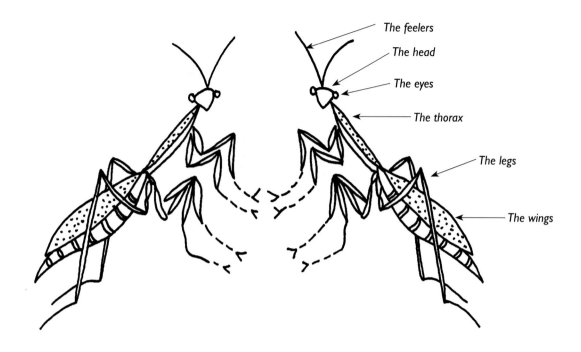

The feelers

The head

The eyes

The thorax

The legs

The wings

Butterflies: organza

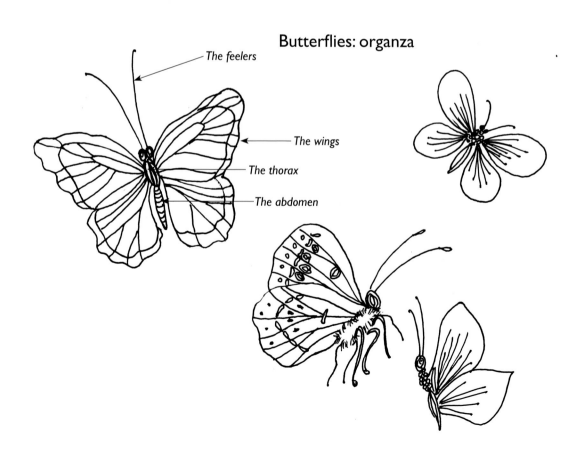

The feelers

The wings

The thorax

The abdomen

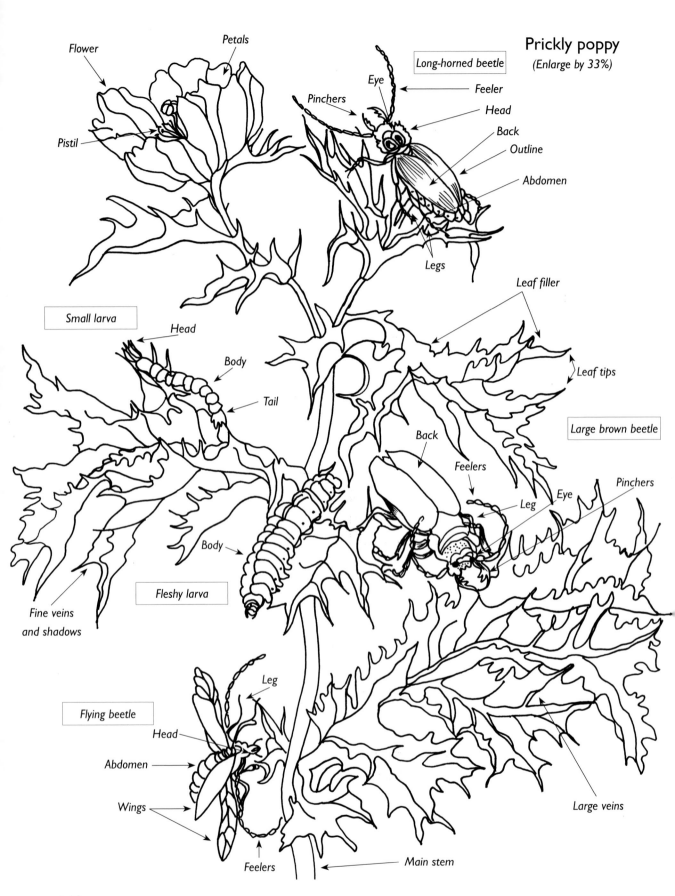

Flower

Petals

Prickly poppy
(Enlarge by 33%)

Long-horned beetle

Eye

Feeler

Pinchers

Head

Back

Outline

Pistil

Abdomen

Legs

Leaf filler

Small larva

Head

Body

Leaf tips

Tail

Large brown beetle

Back

Feelers

Eye

Pinchers

Leg

Body

Fine veins
and shadows

Fleshy larva

Leg

Flying beetle

Head

Abdomen

Wings

Large veins

Feelers

Main stem

Brenton Blue pure silk

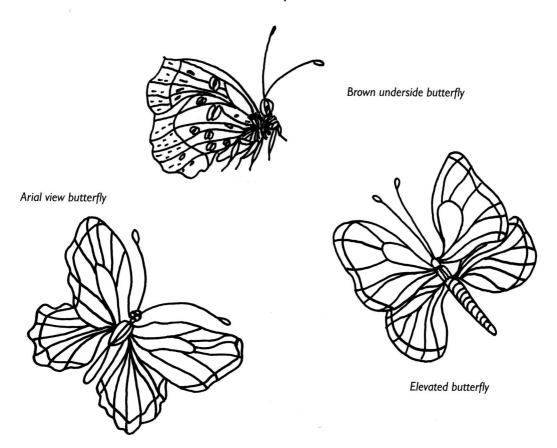

Brown underside butterfly

Arial view butterfly

Elevated butterfly

Dragonfly lampshade or pincushion

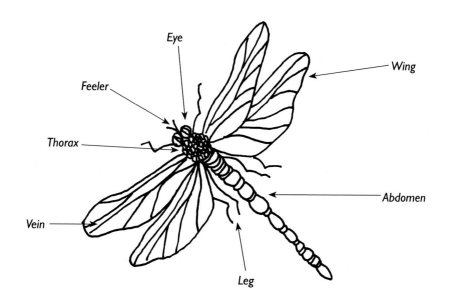

Eye

Wing

Feeler

Thorax

Abdomen

Vein

Leg

Agapanthus africanus

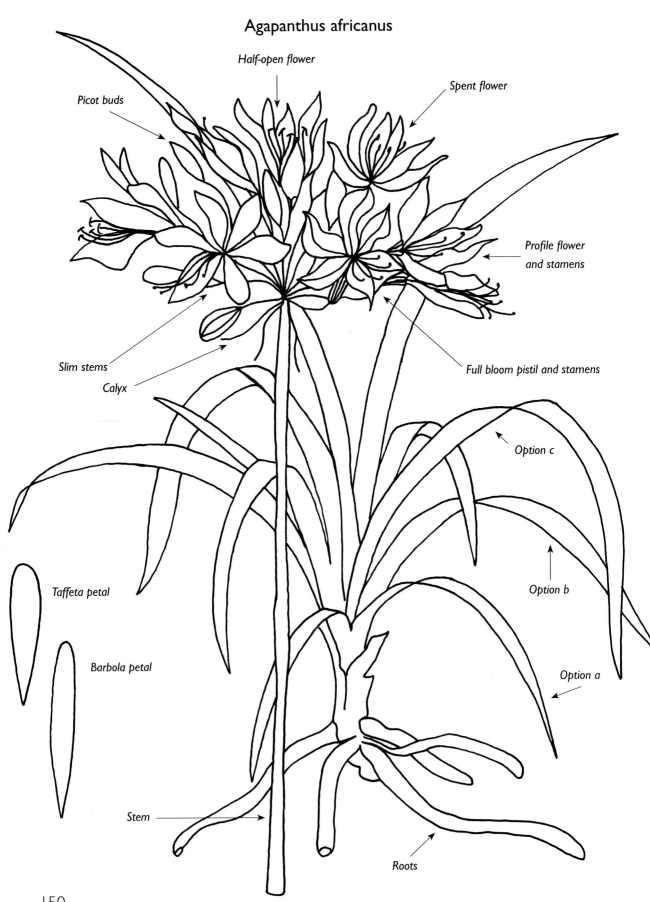

Half-open flower

Spent flower

Picot buds

Profile flower
and stamens

Slim stems

Full bloom pistil and stamens

Calyx

Option c

Option b

Taffeta petal

Option a

Barbola petal

Stem

Roots

150

Hermit crab

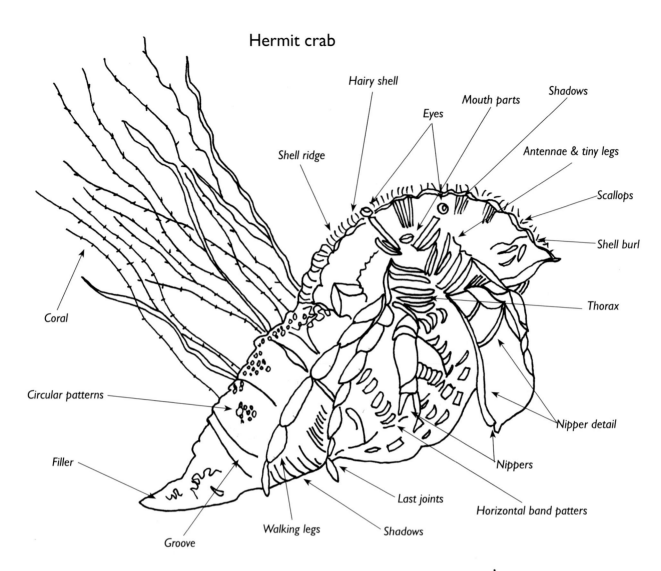

Hairy shell

Mouth parts

Shadows

Eyes

Shell ridge

Antennae & tiny legs

Scallops

Shell burl

Coral

Thorax

Circular patterns

Nipper detail

Filler

Nippers

Groove

Walking legs

Last joints

Shadows

Horizontal band patters

Bouclé beetle

Glorious insects

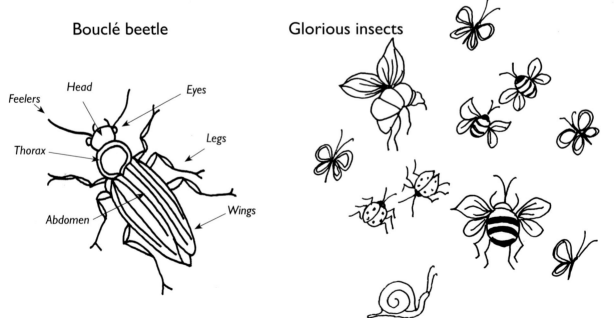

Feelers

Head

Eyes

Thorax

Legs

Abdomen

Wings

Barred owlets

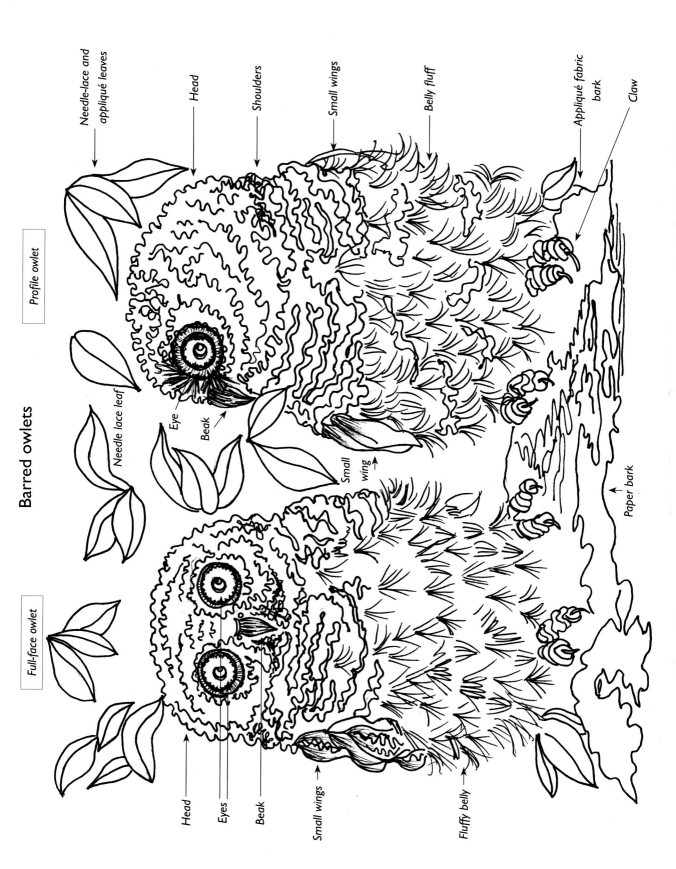

Profile owlet

Needle-lace and appliqué leaves

Head

Shoulders

Small wings

Belly fluff

Appliqué fabric bark

Claw

Needle lace leaf

Eye

Beak

Small wing

Full-face owlet

Head

Eyes

Beak

Small wings

Fluffy belly

Paper bark

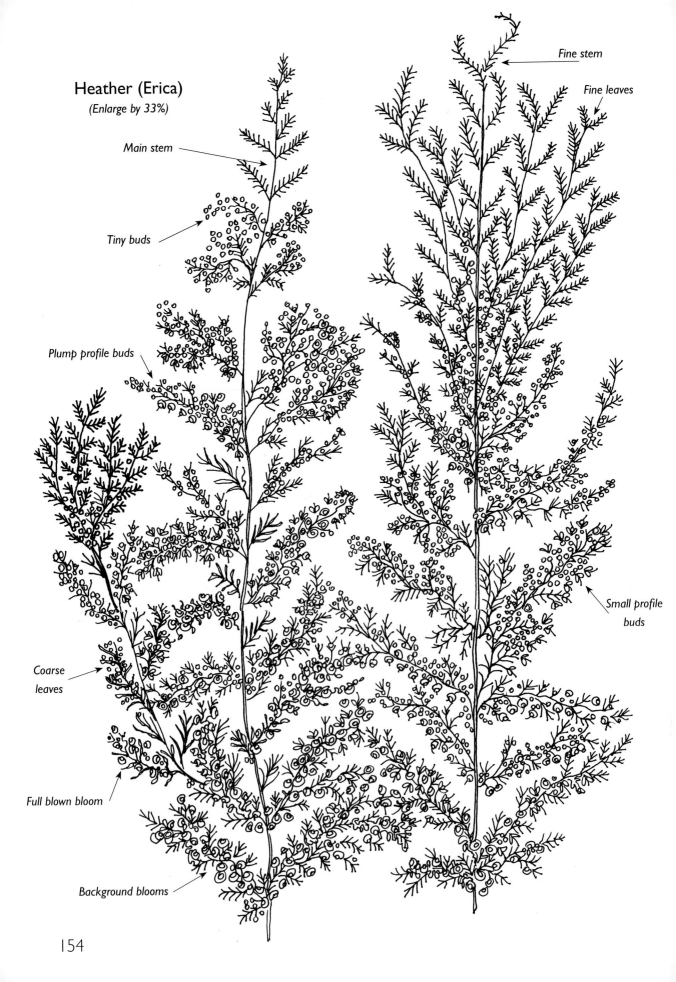

Heather (Erica)
(Enlarge by 33%)

Fine stem

Fine leaves

Main stem

Tiny buds

Plump profile buds

Small profile buds

Coarse leaves

Full blown bloom

Background blooms

154

Pomegranate

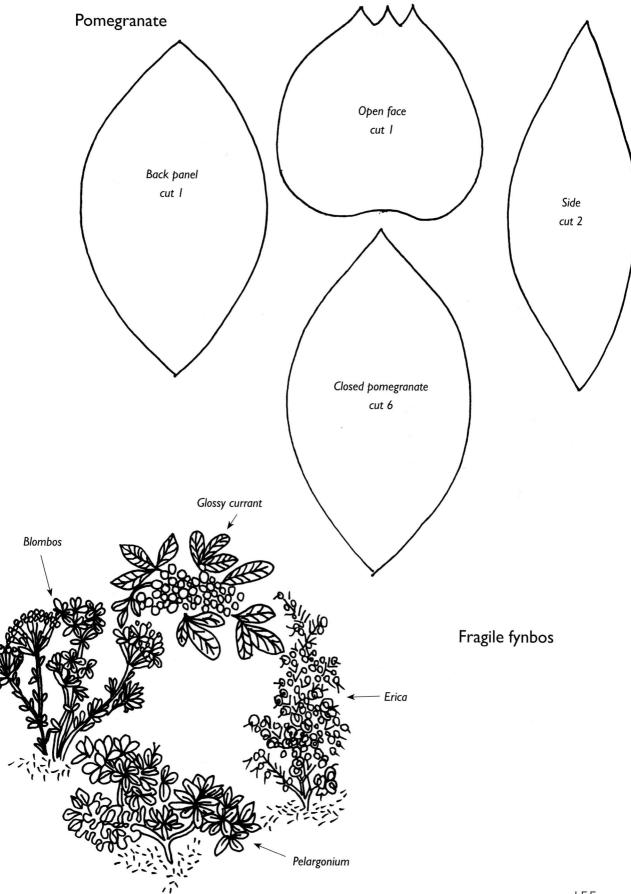

Back panel
cut 1

Open face
cut 1

Side
cut 2

Closed pomegranate
cut 6

Glossy currant

Blombos

Fragile fynbos

Erica

Pelargonium

Burgundy passion flower

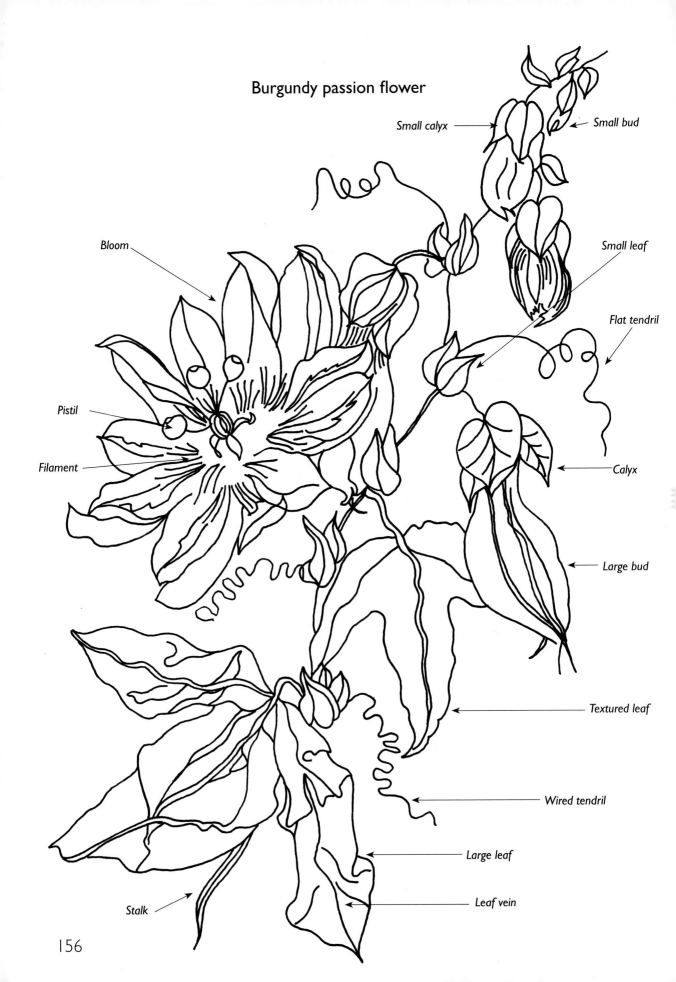

Small calyx

Small bud

Bloom

Small leaf

Flat tendril

Pistil

Calyx

Filament

Large bud

Textured leaf

Wired tendril

Large leaf

Stalk

Leaf vein

African grasshopper

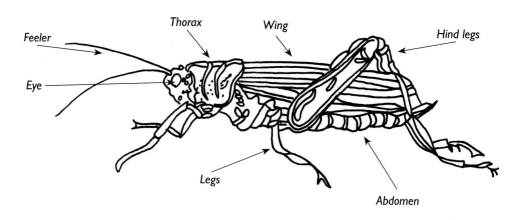

Feeler

Thorax

Wing

Hind legs

Eye

Legs

Abdomen

Grasshopper in motion

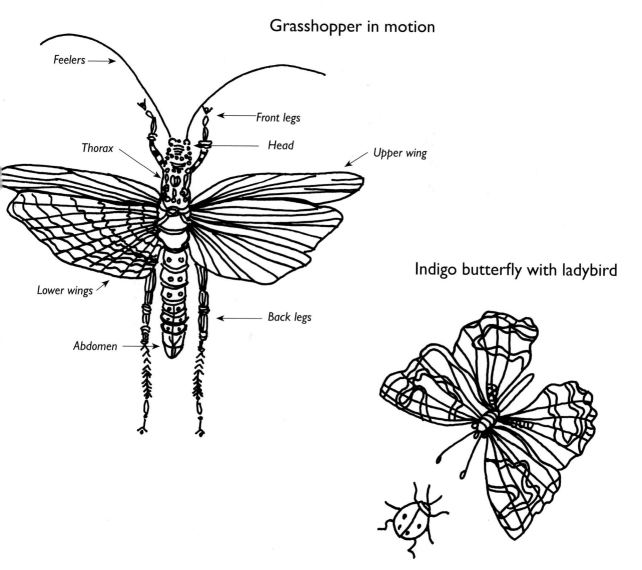

Feelers

Front legs

Thorax

Head

Upper wing

Lower wings

Back legs

Abdomen

Indigo butterfly with ladybird

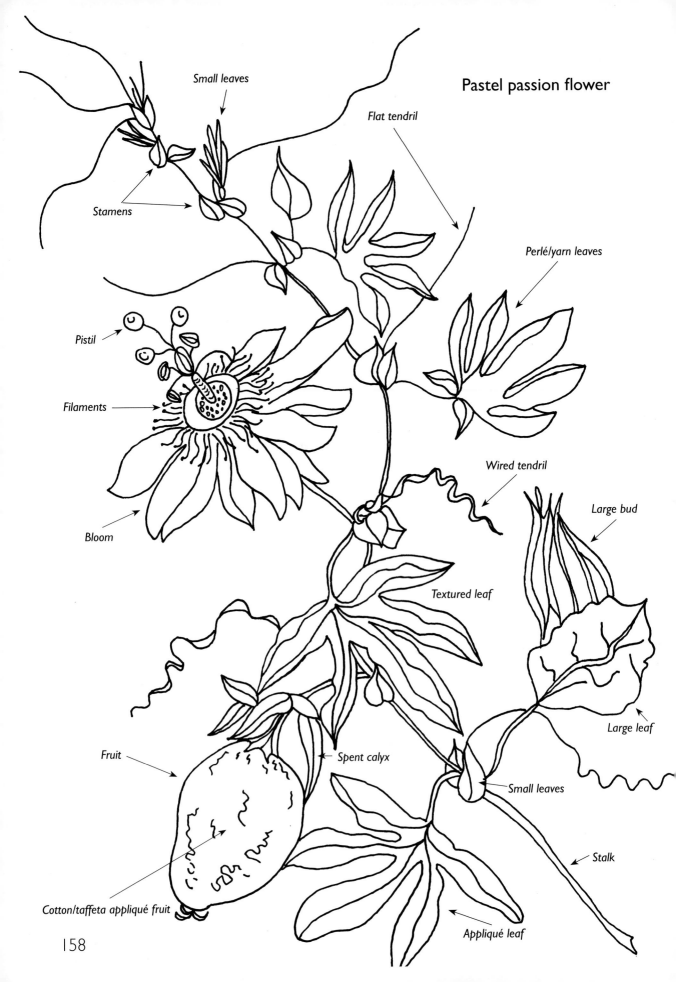

Small leaves

Stamens

Flat tendril

Pastel passion flower

Perlé/yarn leaves

Pistil

Filaments

Bloom

Wired tendril

Large bud

Textured leaf

Large leaf

Fruit

Spent calyx

Small leaves

Stalk

Cotton/taffeta appliqué fruit

Appliqué leaf

3-D Fig

(Enlarge by 33%)

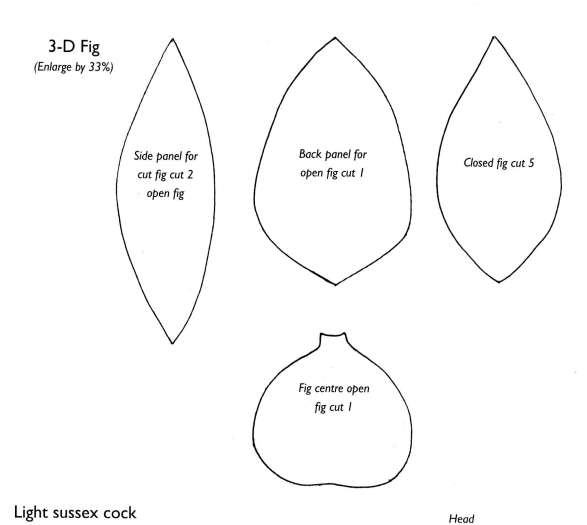

Side panel for
cut fig cut 2
open fig

Back panel for
open fig cut 1

Closed fig cut 5

Fig centre open
fig cut 1

Light sussex cock

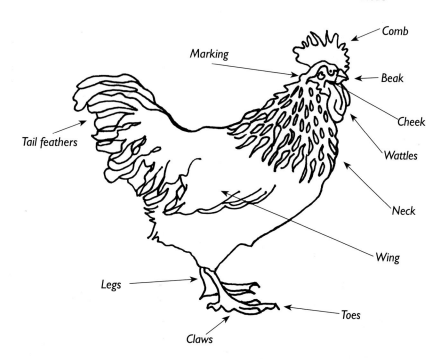

Head

Comb

Marking

Beak

Cheek

Wattles

Tail feathers

Neck

Wing

Legs

Toes

Claws

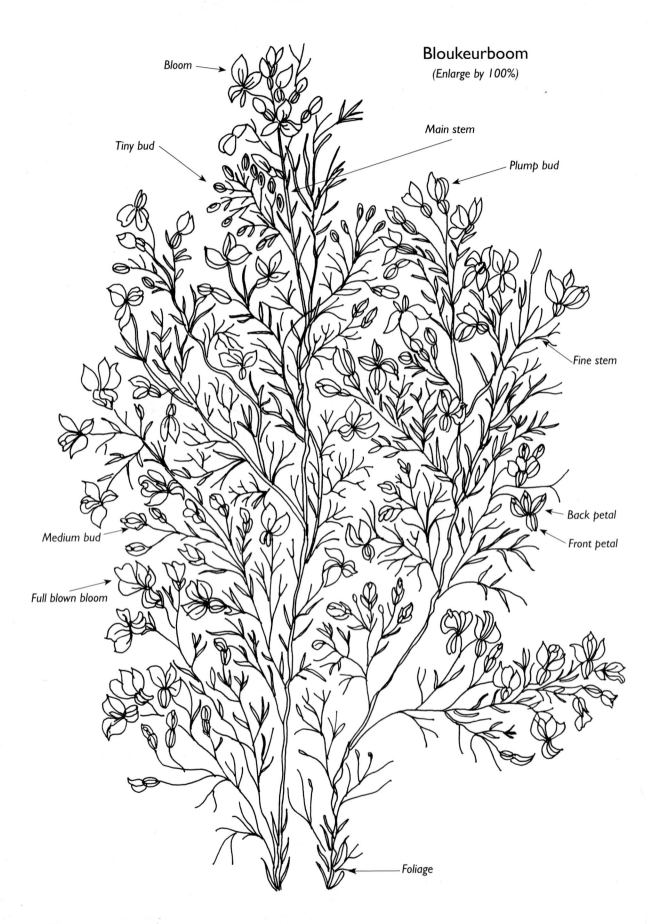

Bloukeurboom
(Enlarge by 100%)

Bloom

Tiny bud

Main stem

Plump bud

Fine stem

Medium bud

Back petal

Front petal

Full blown bloom

Foliage